WHAT WOMEN ARE SAYING ABOUT CAROL TUTTLE'S
Beauty Profile^{SM} SYSTEM AND *DRESSING YOUR TRUTH*®

Thank you for letting me know that I can be me! I've never felt my own sense of self: I've been looking in the mirror for 45 years and not seeing me! Thank you so much for your Beauty Profile^{SM} *and the Dressing Your Truth*® *systems. Now I am seeing the real me more and more each day!* **—MYRA**

Dressing Your Truth® *has given me permission to be me! I like shopping now because I have a purpose and I know what I am looking for.* **—AMANDA**

I now wear more muted colors. To my surprise, my skin looks more alive with those colors! **—ROSIE**

I want to share a wonderful experience I had with my four girls... we all went shopping. We spent the whole day, went to lunch and found lots of bargains. We laughed a lot and enjoyed our new insights about our strengths and challenges within our Types. What a fun and empowering experience it was...[to] support each other in such a positive way... You have made a difference for all of us. **—TERRY**

I have been following Dressing My Truth for almost a year. I get compliments daily! I love knowing what works in my wardrobe. **—JANET**

What a relief to finally know my true self and to stop wasting my money, time and energy on all the wrong things. **—BEA**

I feel so great and look so hot...after completing Dressing Your Truth®, *my closet is filled with clothes I love wearing.* **—SHERRY**

This has been an amazing journey, one I plan on continuing on over my lifetime...my husband has commented daily on how nice I look. One of the most enjoyable things is that I know what I am wearing works and I no longer have to worry about that. **—KELLY**

I have been applying some of the rules for my Type and all I can say is "Wow"—and so does my husband... What is amazing about this is that I really do feel pretty and feminine for the first time in many years. **—ROCHELLE**

How does one give thanks for getting a life back? I feel like the fire inside is beginning to glow. Thank you for the leading out, doing what you do and being your authentic self. You've been so instrumental in the transformation of many. **—NANCY**

DRESSING *Your* TRUTH®

Discover Your Type of Beauty

CAROL TUTTLE

Best-selling author of
Remembering Wholeness and *It's Just My Nature!*

LIVE YOUR TRUTH

PRESS

Dressing Your Truth®, Beauty Profile℠, Energy Profiling®,
Body Profiling℠, Energy Type℠, Energy Draping℠, and Type 1℠,
Type 2℠, Type 3℠, and Type 4℠
are trademarks or registered trademarks of
Carol Tuttle Enterprises, LLC.

1st Printing 2010
2nd Printing 2011
3rd Printing 2012
4th Printing 2nd Edition 2013
5th Printing 3rd Edition February 2014

ISBN-10: 0-9844021-0-1
ISBN-13: 978-0-9844021-0-6

Library of Congress Control Number: 2010920375

Cover photo by Debra Macfarlane
(www.debramacfarlane.com)
Cover and text design by Tara Mayberry
(www.teaberrycreative.com)

support@liveyourtruth.com
www.liveyourtruth.com

Clothes should look as if
a woman was born into them.

—GEOFFREY BEENE

OTHER BOOKS FROM CAROL TUTTLE

The Path to Wholeness

*Remembering Wholeness: A Personal Handbook for
Thriving in the 21st Century*

*It's Just My Nature! A Guide to Knowing and Living Your
True Nature*

*The Child Whisperer: The Ultimate Handbook for Raising
Happy, Successful, Cooperative Children*

DEDICATED TO THE WOMEN OF THE WORLD.

MAY YOU ALL DISCOVER

YOUR GREATEST BEAUTY,

AND LIVE IT TO THE FULLEST,

INSIDE AND OUT!

Acknowledgements

I WOULD LIKE TO THANK THE MANY WOMEN who have shown up in my life to teach me that every woman is innately beautiful.

Thank you to my daughters, Jennifer and Anne. You have learned your true natures and beauty at an early age, and this knowledge will serve you well your entire life. Thank you to my daughters-in-law, Sarah and Jaleah who have embraced my teachings whole-heartedly and brought out their beauty to share with the world.

Thank you to my sons Chris, Mark and Mario, and my sons-in-law, Tony and Tanner. Your example to other men of how to support the beautiful women in your life is so admirable.

Thank you to my great husband, Jonathan—you continue to support and love my passions for dreaming and living big.

Thank you to my team, the people who have come and gone in this journey and the team members who continue to support the worldwide vision we hold to help every woman know her truth and dress it! My husband Jonathan, my son Chris, my son-in-law Tanner, my daughter Anne, and daughter-in-law Sarah are the core members of my team, and they are each invaluable in the roles they play in building our business.

Also, thanks to: our graphic designer, Tim Kavmark, who continues to share his genius with us; our film and production crew including Marcy Brown, Kent Findlay, Anna K Findlay, Samantha Butterworth, and Tanner Christensen who took what had previously only been taught at live events and created world-class online learning courses so women worldwide could learn how to dress their truth; and to Mike Fitzgerald who edited this book.

I have a passion to revolutionize the beauty and fashion world, and to help women all over the world take back their beauty. I acknowledge you for finding and reading this book, and becoming the next woman to discover the secrets to her true beauty and learn how to use the tools to express your beauty almost effortlessly and with growing confidence.

TABLE OF CONTENTS

INTRODUCTION

I AM VERY EXCITED TO INTRODUCE YOU to a program that I am incredibly passionate about, a program that has changed my life forever as well as the lives of thousands of other women. It's called the *Beauty Profile*^SM system, and it is the very first step to *Dressing Your Truth*®. The *Beauty Profile*^SM system is not focused on putting beauty on, but on your inner source of beauty—the real you. What you will learn is that your outer beauty truly starts with your inner beauty, and when you know the truth about your inner beauty—your unique Type of beauty—you will be ready to adorn your body to show your true beauty through your outer appearance.

For many women, dressing and adorning themselves has been one of the biggest challenges of their lives, a lifelong battle that started when they were in their young teens. Most women feel defeated by that battle because, based on the way the fashion world works, it seems to be a battle you can never win. We have blamed ourselves and our looks for not looking great in the clothes that we are lured to purchase by a fashion culture with an insatiable appetite for trends and change. Fortunately, you are going to discover in the pages of this book how misinformed we have been and how unnecessarily hard we have been on ourselves for something that quite frankly, until now, you have not had the tools to change.

The *Beauty Profiling*^SM system will teach you a new way of looking at yourself, not just for today but for a lifetime. It will put you in touch with your intuitive sense of which fashions are right for you, what looks best on you, and what you are naturally and instinctively drawn to.

Knowing your personal Type of beauty will not only set the stage for you to experience the *Dressing Your Truth*® system, it will give you a deeper and clearer understanding of who you are—your unique gifts and talents, your inherent qualities and traits, why you are the Type of woman that you are. This will support you in moving forward in your life in great confidence and awareness. In this day and age, we as women are ready to know ourselves more fully and clearly and to live it with honesty and confidence.

My goal for you is that after reading this book you will be able to say, "I know what my personal Type of beauty is, and I know now that my life will be different forever! I love myself!"

The purpose of this book is to assist you in discovering your personal Type of beauty. Once you know your Type of beauty and what Type of woman you are, you will be ready to learn how to dress your truth. You will not learn what clothes, jewelry, accessories, makeup, skincare, and hairstyles are perfect for you by reading this book. In fact, I don't think anyone should learn a fashion and beauty system only through a book. I have studied dozens of fashion and beauty books, and to me, they are too often a maze of captions and pictures, difficult to put into the kind of practical application that creates any satisfying results.

You can create your total personal makeover with the extensive video course and resources at www.dressingyourtruth.com. Here you will find online learning courses and support materials for each Type of beauty. The fashion world has avoided giving you the tools to understand and dress for your Type of beauty, but *Dressing Your Truth*® specializes in giving you hands-on tools to teach you what clothes will look best on you, the best color, cut and style for your hair, how to apply makeup to look naturally beautiful, what jewelry to wear and how to accessorize an outfit in a style that is perfect for you. Where the fashion world left you guessing, *Dressing Your Truth®* makes you your own beauty expert.

Our site is the first website of its kind. There are no other online learning courses about beauty that go into as much detail, that have as many informative how-tos and have as many exceptional videos and images, that teach you all you need to know to look your very best. Thousands of women have already benefited from this easy-to-use online learning portal. By offering this material, we also have created a community of beauty-conscious women who love and support each other through our community forums and live regular *Dressing Your Truth®* Club Night broadcasts where we continue to teach and support you.

In the *Dressing Your Truth®* community, I marvel at how incredibly supportive and loving women are when they know their inner truth and feel confident and secure in their appearance. All the earlier feelings of being less than adequate and beautiful—which set us up to feel threatened and even jealous of attractive women—start to disappear when we dress our truth, and the camaraderie of the true feminine nature emerges to show love and support for one another in being our most beautiful selves.

I will be referring to this website frequently in this book as this book and the courses and resources are meant to be experienced together. In today's world of advanced technology, it only makes sense to combine the written word with online, interactive, visual learning tools to give the optimal learning experience. After taking the *Dressing Your Truth®* course, you will have the tools and insights you need to know what to buy, how to accessorize your clothes, how to get the best look for you with makeup and be the expert for your own hair.

I am excited for you to start this journey. No matter your age, size, or color, every woman deserves to be beautiful!

Part 1

IT STARTED WITH TWIGGY:
MY PERSONAL BEAUTY NIGHTMARE

MY STORY IS LIKE MOST WOMEN'S STORIES when it comes to fashion and beauty. It is not a very fun story.

For most of my life, I hated my body and struggled with how I looked. Even so, at age 45 I finally discovered the tools that allowed me to love and appreciate my body and my looks. I'm about to tell you how. But first, let me tell you about my beginnings.

Around age 12, I started to notice that what I wore and how I looked became very important. I was an attractive girl that was pretty much left to myself to figure out how to put clothes together, wear makeup, and so on. But I lay no fault at the feet of my mom. I believe she did the best she knew how, and I can't imagine that I made it easy for her to convey her beauty secrets to me—which I now know would not have been right for my Type of beauty. I had no sisters to seek advice from and my brothers, well, they thought girlie stuff was pretty much a waste of time.

By age 13, I had very thick, bushy, "boyish" eyebrows. And I hated them. True to my Type 3, determined nature, I took swift action and removed most of my eyebrows in one evening with a pair of tweezers and a bathroom mirror. I had no help and no instruction, which was readily apparent by the looks of my eyebrows once I was done.

Not knowing any better, I assumed this new look was an improvement, that is until I hit my seventh period band class where a boy next to me looked at me in horror and exclaimed, "What happened to your eyebrows?" That moment was an initiation to many years of believing that I was not attractive enough, not thin enough, and not pretty enough.

About this same time my three brothers and their friends added their two cents by shamelessly teasing me with the nickname "Carol Barrel," and comments like "Hey, peg legs!" and "Crater face!" Needless to say, that did not help in my opinion of my looks and body image.

By high school, I had made little progress and was doing what most girls were doing—buying and trying to wear what was in fashion (except miniskirts—I just could not pour my larger size frame into the Twiggy fashions that were the rage). My battle with weight and hatred for my body really kicked in at age 15, which went on to last 30 more years. I had little confidence inwardly and disgust with myself because I believed I was overweight on the outside.

> I PRETENDED LIKE EVERY OTHER GIRL PRETENDED, HIDING MY SHAME FOR MY BODY AND LOOKS

I never liked how I looked, and I felt increasingly uncomfortable in my clothes. I pretended pretty much like every other girl pretended, hiding my shame for my body and looks and pretending I felt good about myself. By age 17, my shopping and dressing room experiences were a nightmare. I had gained an excess of 30 pounds at this point and created an eating disorder of binging and—oh, but I forgot the purging part, so I just kept gaining weight.

Now put this picture together: a teenage girl, 30 pounds overweight, who had been introduced to the fashion world five years earlier when the first supermodel and British fashion icon was a 91-pound teenage girl. Her name was Twiggy. Remember her?

Guess who didn't like herself, her looks, and her body at all? You got it: me! I hated my body, I hated how I looked, and had completely no self-confidence in my teenage, female self.

I hated trying on clothes and had many an argument with my Type 2, gentle-natured mother who was more than confused on how to help me. I started a pattern of being late for school, since I tried outfit after outfit on in the morning trying to find something I felt halfway decent in. My mom finally insisted I pick out my clothes the night before, which only gave me more time to try it on, hate it, and berate myself even more. I told myself that my body and outward appearance was inferior.

After years of this inner struggle, off to college I went, and for the first time in my life, at age 18, I found a makeup class at a local salon in the college town I lived in. I signed up for a personal consultation, and went to learn about how to put on makeup from someone who I figured knew better than me what was right on me. In spite of what help I got (or did not get) from the makeup class, my battle with food, body image and low self-esteem continued.

Fortunately, I met a man that loved me for who I was at the time. I married Jon Tuttle when I was 22 years old, just 4 days after my university graduation.

On to marriage and motherhood and the next 23 years of doing my best to look my best, still being influenced by fashion trends and styles, but never feeling I looked great in them. I had the perm in the 80s, the black in the 90s and started to discover my true beauty in the 2000s!

For 33 years of my life, I fell prey to the belief that, like most every woman out there, my inability to look great in what was in fashion was all my fault, and there was little I could do about it.

THE SUPERMODEL STANDARD

Unfortunately, for most of my life, all of my efforts in beautifying myself were an effort to improve what I thought was originally flawed. My natural type of beauty is not found in the modern day world of fashion and beauty. In fact, my type of physical features would be deemed as aged and masculine.

If it weren't for *Dressing Your Truth*®, I may have never discovered my own unique beauty. At this phase in my life, I am incredibly grateful that I can look past the current trend of anti-aging techniques and products as necessities for being beautiful.

Actually, it wasn't until I started to develop *Dressing Your Truth*® that I became interested in the fashion and beauty world. But not for the common reasons most women would: my reasons were to find the faults and failures in the current system that had played a huge role in affecting my degrading opinion of myself as a woman.

As I mentioned earlier, at age 12 I began to look to the outside world, and the fashion and beauty world, as the reference to my developing womanhood. Because the beauty icon of the time was a 91-pound blonde Type 4 female with the name Twiggy, I would bet it is safe to say not many girls had a chance at feeling beautiful. Twiggy was the first of a long line of women who set the standard of beauty that we call supermodels.

Ladies, it has been 40 years that we have been judging ourselves as women against a "supermodel standard" that we can never measure up to. The standard of a very tall, thin sleek woman that appears much younger than she is—that's what we have come to consider beautiful. And to make matters worse, with all the photo enhancing and airbrushing that now takes place in the media, the superficial beauty we pit ourselves against can only perpetuate a deep inner sense of failure in the effort to feel beautiful as a woman.

The Dove Campaign for Real Beauty (see www.dove.us) was started after Dove did a worldwide study on beauty called The Real Truth About Beauty: A World Report. The Dove report confirmed their premise that the common definition for beauty had become impossible for most women to attain. The study pointed out only 2 percent—yes, 2 PERCENT—of women considered themselves beautiful, and only 12 percent of women said they were "very satisfied" with their physical attractiveness. On the other end of the scale, 75 percent of the women who responded wished that the media did a more responsible job of portraying the diversity of women's physical attractiveness, including size and shape, across all ages.

I'm sure you probably agree with the 75 percent of women who wished the media would take a different approach. It's time we all took a different approach to beauty.

WHERE I AM NOW ON MY JOURNEY

At the time of this writing, I am in my early fifties and I honestly feel and believe that I look hot! In fact, I know I have never looked better! I love how I look, and I feel confident that what I am wearing is perfect for me. I love to shop and find the pieces that are just right for me. The best part, now that I know how to dress my truth, is that shopping is a breeze. I find what I want fast and what I find is always affordable.

My biggest challenge is no longer wondering what to wear but asking myself, "What great outfit should I wear today!" I know the best color, cut, and style for my hair. I know how to do it every day so I never have a bad hair day. I no longer worry that my body is too big, or whether my butt looks big. I no longer look in a dressing room mirror with disgust thinking I can't look good until I lose 20 pounds. I look in the mirror and love what I see. I don't have to ask my husband or my friends "Does this look good on me?" because I know what looks good and I buy it with confidence.

Seven years ago, I started to take back my beauty. I have taken it back and love owning it and sharing it. True to my Type 3, ambitious nature, I have built a business out of what I have discovered to help women all over the world take back their beauty.

I have spent years in healing my wounded feminine self. As you will discover when you read further in this book, I am a Type 3 woman. I have learned that because I repressed my rich, dynamic

Type 3 expression for most of my life, it was the cause of my lack of self-esteem. Discovering my Type and allowing myself to live it and dress it has brought me a whole new life, even in my middle years.

I am grateful for my journey. It is due to my own experience that I have come to understand yours.

As my daughter Anne recently shared with me, "Mom, if you had not gone through what you have, you would have never created all the great resources you have that are helping people all over the world!" This is true—thanks for the reminder, Anne!

Because I know how my journey has turned out, I know how yours can turn out, too. Let's get started in taking back your true nature and true beauty so you too can look in the mirror and love what you see, and most importantly, feel the love you have for yourself.

How The Fashion World Has Failed Women

AFTER READING THIS SECTION you might just say to yourself, "Why didn't I think of that? It makes total sense!"

The fashion world has failed us because the system of ever-changing fashion trends and styles does not give us the tools we need to bring out our greatest beauty as women. However, the ever-changing fashion trends do work to create demand—demand to purchase the latest fashions—in women who do not know what works best for them, or what they really want, which is likely the majority of women in the Western world.

Think about it for a moment. From the beginning of recorded history, fashion has separated those who have money from those who have little or no money, and thereby created social classes—separation and lack and envy and turned-up noses.

The fashion world is built on a system of ever changing fashions and trends. Who in the world thought that the latest fashion trend could look great on every woman? But many women are willing to pay for the illusion that they will look good in those fashions.

Styles and trends don't make a woman beautiful. If anything, they are interfering with and taking away your beauty. Since we all have different bodies, face shapes, and personalities, we can't all look great in the same clothes. Fashion trends and styles are designed to honor the clothes, not the woman.

If you look better in more stylized, structured design lines and fabrication but the latest trend is soft, flowy fabrications with soft design lines, you are not going to look beautiful: you are going to look frumpy and feel frumpy.

Fashion magazines have become a form of entertainment, and in some cases bizarre art, showing women in outfits that the everyday woman would never wear. They depict women that are not real, invented by air brushing and photo editing.

The fashion system has not and will never even attempt to teach us the skills and tools to honor our true nature and our unique physical traits so we can become our own beauty expert. Rather, it has left us guessing, shaming ourselves into being the problem, and keeping us on the treadmill of chasing the latest trends, only to buy more clothes with more and more uncertainty.

The current fashion system teaches us how to put on beauty, not how to bring out our true beauty. I've learned that when you are feeling insecure about how you look, and trying to put on your look or trying to put on your beauty, you can be very intimidated by other women, especially by one who is looking naturally amazing and beautiful. These insecurities get stirred up when you're still trying to put beauty on. You can't put on beauty unless it reflects the beauty you recognize inside yourself.

> YOU CAN'T PUT ON BEAUTY UNLESS IT REFLECTS THE BEAUTY YOU RECOGNIZE INSIDE YOURSELF.

When you see a woman who looks fashionable, you are usually seeing a woman who is putting beauty on. You see the clothes first, then the woman! When you see a woman dressing her truth, you see the woman first, then the inspiring ensemble of clothing, jewelry, makeup, and hair supporting her real nature. What she has on her body looks like a natural extension of her true self, her true beauty.

I believe very few women care passionately about fashion, but I believe every woman deeply cares about being beautiful, inside and out.

Even television shows that feature makeovers and fashion help are not helping. One of the most popular in the United States is called "What Not to Wear." The basis of the show is making over a woman who is fashion-challenged and who needs help improving her overall style and appearance. It is common that the clients they work with on this show look like they really need help—they are either out-of-date with their look or just don't put much time or effort into their appearance. They go to the woman's house and tear apart her closet, ruthlessly shaming her choices in the process of removing most of the clothes she owns. It is not apparent to me that they give her much in the way of practical guidance or tools to go shopping with, but they do provide her with a $5,000 budget to rebuild her wardrobe.

First off, how many of us can set aside $5,000 to overhaul our closet? I don't know any woman who watches "What Not to Wear" who is raving about how many great shopping tips she has gotten out of it, nor do I know any in whom the show has instilled great confidence that what she is wearing is perfect for her.

Shows like this are really another form of fashion entertainment, with little practical value for the everyday woman. Personally, I can't watch it. I get too frustrated seeing what they are doing in their effort to put beauty on the woman. To tell you the truth, I would love to do a *Dressing Your Truth*® makeover after their makeover!

HATING HOW YOU LOOK

As I was going through some old pictures to find the images I wanted to share in this book, I was startled by something I discovered. As I mentioned earlier, I hated how boyish my thick, bold, bushy eyebrows made me look when I was in seventh grade. Much to my surprise, since I had forgotten what I was about to see, when I came across my picture in my seventh grade yearbook, I was shocked at what I saw. I had taken a pen and completely scratched out my image! The picture of me was taken before I had my private eyebrow-plucking session.

The disdain and embarrassment I felt for trying to make my boyish looks more feminine was very powerfully witnessed to me by this act of scratching out my picture when I was 13. I really did hate how I looked. Looking back and reflecting on this now—almost 40 years later—brought me to tears and got me even more fired up to change what we do to ourselves as women and to expose where the fault lies.

Let me say this really clearly: the fault does not lie with us as women. It is in the system of fashion and beauty that we have blindly accepted and have been convinced is acceptable since our pre-teen days. We have not paused to question it. It is like a slow, torturous drip of false programming that starts in a female's life somewhere between the ages of 10 and 13. It sets us up to believe that if we don't look and feel good in the current trends and styles, the fault is in our body and physical appearance, not in the system itself.

When I came across pictures of myself at 15, when I weighed 150 pounds, I was also surprised and shocked. I saw myself in a whole new light. I was not overweight by reasonable, healthy standards. Yes, I had a more athletic build and was more muscular (definitely not the skinny girl) but what I saw was a perfectly healthy teenage girl!

I am convinced that my imbalanced belief and perception at that stage was the catalyst to develop an eating disorder in the next couple of years, which ultimately caused me to gain more weight. If I had had a healthy view of myself then, sustained by sound beliefs, I never would have developed those patterns and likely would have avoided 30 years of body image despair.

Like most girls, I accepted these false beliefs about my body image and appearance that were based on the media-based fashion and beauty standards. I compared myself to them, like most other girls, and fully accepted the lie that I was not thin enough or pretty enough and that it was my fault. I now know the standard I measured myself against was seriously flawed.

MARY'S STORY

Mary is a client of mine. Her story is a great example of how the current system of fashion has failed us. Mary's struggle is all too familiar to many women. Read her story and see how big the transformation has been in her life match your personal Type of beauty and how to dress her truth.

"I was asked how my life was different after I participated in Dressing Your Truth®, after I changed how I wear my hair, makeup and clothes…. One thing I noticed right away is that shopping is no longer my nightmare. I used to dread shopping. It took hours of trying on things to find even one item I could tolerate.

"Now, I don't try on anything that isn't in my five elements from Dressing Your Truth®! It takes me only a few minutes to sort through a rack and see if there's even anything worth trying on. And when I do try something on, it's almost always a keeper. No more frustrating two-hour dressing room sessions where everything I put on looks terrible and makes me feel terrible about myself.

"Now shopping is easy and fast. And I love my new clothes. That benefit alone would have made the Dressing Your Truth® training totally worth it. But there's so much more. I had a very positive reaction from my family and coworkers about my new look, but the important part of this transformation has been internal, not external. I wish I could articulate this better—but the difference is in how I feel and how I approach people and situations. I am more confident, more able to function in my workplace and home environment because I feel better, lighter and more energetic. It is as if a weight has been lifted.

"I never realized how all the black and the harsh, stark lines I wore made me feel. It doesn't seem rational that this material or that material or this color or that color could make a difference about how I feel and present myself, but it does. When I am in clothes that are dynamic and rich in color and texture, I feel happier.

"When I feel happier, I make better presentations, I interact with clients and students more positively, and others who don't know me more quickly accept me. I work in the education sector where, among other things, I work with teachers to produce materials, negotiate contracts, and work out difficulties with students and parents. I used to have to take five or ten minutes talking to a new faculty member or student or parent to convince them that I both knew what I was talking about and was truly concerned for their well-being and able to do the job at hand. Now I have noticed that the acceptance happens much more quickly. It is as if the fact that how I look and the energy I carry harmonize and set others at ease even before I attempt to help them feel at ease with my words. And that has made all the difference in the world. The results have been incredible. Thank you for this training."

Where the fashion world has failed you, *Dressing Your Truth*® will honor you. After you discover what Type of woman you are with my *Beauty Profile*SM system, adapted from my groundbreaking *Energy Profiling*® system, you will be ready to learn how to Dress Your Truth. *Dressing Your Truth*® is a simple system that teaches you the five elements that match your personal Type of beauty.

I could tell you many stories just like Mary's, from women all over the world. Every woman deserves to look beautiful every day of their lives, and now they can have the tools to accomplish that goal effortlessly, affordably and joyfully.

The world of fashion has failed us and shamed us long enough. You no longer need to believe that you are the problem because you are not. I am confident in saying that once you learn how to dress your truth, you will own your beauty and personal fashion and dress with confidence and success. Where the fashion system left you guessing on what to buy, you will know each and every time you go shopping what is perfect for you. I fully expect that you will have your own success story just like Mary's!

DOES THIS MAKE MY BUTT LOOK BIG?

YOU'VE HEARD YOURSELF SAY IT. You've gone shopping with your girlfriends and you've heard them ask it. Growing up, you probably heard your mom say it, too! "Does this make my butt look big?" My mom said it a lot when I was a kid. In fact, I can remember being somewhere in public with my mom pointing to another woman's behind and whispering to me, "Is my butt as big as hers?" Being the loving, dutiful daughter that I am, of course I said no!

Women have struggled with negative body images for decades. Our mothers taught us to be self-conscious about our bodies with their negative image of theirs. The media has taught us that unless we are super slim, we are not acceptable.

A recent question on ChaCha (www.chacha.com) was, "What's the average dress size for women in America?" The answer? The average size woman in America is a size 12, not a size 6! However, the average mannequin is a size 6. Is it any surprise that 44 percent of women who are of average weight think that they are overweight?

I remember when I weighed in at 150 pounds when I was 15 years old, and I thought I was as fat as a pig! When compared to 91 pound Twiggy, any 150 pound teen girl would perceive herself as fat. I can't even remember weighing 91 pounds! Possibly in the third grade I weighed that much, but I wasn't concerned about my weight and body image when I was 10 years old, so I am sure I never even weighed myself! I carried the impression of being extremely overweight for the next three decades. Every time I weighed myself, I shamed myself. Negative body image is a chronic problem in most women's minds, no matter where they live in the world.

Have you ever considered that the clothes you are wearing are adding to your negative body image by making your body appear bigger than it is? Isn't it a reasonable concern that we may be adding pounds and inches to our behinds just by wearing the wrong clothes? It is!

But how do we know what's going to make our butts look bigger than they really are? If I could share with you a formula for dressing that not only made sure your butt never looked bigger than it is, and in fact it made it look smaller, and this formula gave you the skill set to look like a "10" every day of your life, would you want to know about it? I would think so! No woman wants her butt to look big!

Most clothing systems out there emphasize one thing: color. What I have learned from creating *Dressing Your Truth*® is there is a lot more to a garment than just color. In fact, I have made it easy for you. There are actually four other elements that create a garment that either add to our natural beauty or conflict with it that every garment has. These elements are design line, texture, fabrication, pattern, and of course, chroma/color.

If you are not wearing the right design line, texture, fabrication or pattern that honors the natural movement and beauty of you, I don't care what color your pants are, your butt is going to look bigger than it really is.

It is really simple. Knowing the five elements of dressing that are right for your Type of beauty makes shopping and wardrobing a no-brainer. I have taught this formula to thousands of women and I want to teach it to you, so you never have to ask the question again, "Does this make my butt look big?"

And just so you know, since I have been dressing my truth in my five elements, I can't remember the last time I asked that question, because I know my butt looks great in the clothes that are a "10" for me!

It's Time to Take Back Your Beauty

I SAY THIS WHOLE-HEARTEDLY: most women do not know how truly beautiful they are. Frankly, they have never had the tools to discover their innate beauty or to express it effortlessly.

Most women hear compliments like, "That's a nice jacket" or "I like your purse!" But after learning how to dress their truth, our clients consistently hear compliments like, "You look amazing!"

Is this what you are experiencing now?

- You look in the mirror and say, "Who is that? Is that me? I look terrible!" And the older you get, the more you are feeling this!

- It drives you crazy to get dressed in the morning because you can't decide what looks good on you.

- You look in your closet at the beginning of the day and say, "I haven't the foggiest notion what to put on today!"

- You have a closet full of clothes and only really love a few items.

- You despise clothes shopping because you can't find the right color, or what fits or feels right to you, or what you can afford.

- You go into convulsions at the thought of stepping into a dressing room.

- The compliments you hear may be nice but deep down you feel like they are obligatory.

Once you start dressing your truth, these experiences will no longer be regular occurrence. Why? Because you'll love the way you look, every day. You'll totally enjoy dressing in the morning, and will do so with great confidence. You'll love to shop for clothes because you will always know exactly what you are looking for and what works for you. It will be fun to step into a dressing room again. And you will hear genuine compliments—in fact, they will become an everyday experience.

Just a few days ago, Julie (Type 1) posted this on my Facebook wall. "I went to my profession's bi-annual conference yesterday. My friends haven't seen me since the last conference and since I have started dressing my truth. Boy, did I get the attention—like I have never received! One friend after another couldn't stop mentioning how great I looked. I had one friend say specifically as she couldn't stop staring, 'Your make-up just "pops"!' I had to silently laugh because what you say about the compliments we would hear is right on. Of course, I told them to go to your website to learn more. Once again Carol Tuttle is right."

YOU HAVE BEEN UNDERSTATING YOURSELF AND SETTLING FOR MEDIOCRITY IN YOUR APPEARANCE MOST OF YOUR LIFE.

I receive emails like the one below every day from women who are falling in love with their appearance and their body, and they are not even at their ideal weight! Pamela shares:

"Today was the first time my friends saw me dressing my truth and no less than six people at church today stopped me to say how amazing I looked. I love this stuff. I had to see it to believe it, and I sure do now. It also helped me to deal very effectively with a very challenging situation and I never lost my cool, my dignity or my focus. I think feeling so secure in my skin made a big difference for the better. Thank you."

Because many of you are not used to being noticed for your beauty, this may feel awkward and uncomfortable. It is common for women to share with me this sentiment, "I am afraid that dressing my truth will be too much. I am going to stand out."

I tell women to consider the possibility that *Dressing Your Truth*® and bringing out your beauty is not over-stating yourself; consider, rather, that you have been understating yourself and settling for mediocrity in your appearance most of your life.

It is time to take back your beauty and become your own beauty expert. You really don't know how naturally beautiful you are. I have personally witnessed personally witnessed hundreds of women who have shed tears of appreciation when they looked in the mirror and saw for the first time how beautiful they truly are.

I want you to be the next woman to fall in love with herself and to love your body just the way it is right now! Amazing things happen when you feel the true love you really do have for yourself. I am excited for you.

WHAT DRESSING YOUR TRUTH® IS NOT

A LOT OF WOMEN WHO COME INTO THE DRESSING YOUR TRUTH® world have come through or been exposed to other beauty and fashion makeover systems. I can honestly say that *Dressing Your Truth®* is new and unique and cannot be compared to the other systems that have preceded it. *Dressing Your Truth®* is *not*:

- A color-only typing system

- A body shape or body type system, such as rectangular, pear-shapes, hourglass and so forth

- A system where your skin tone and hair color determines what looks good on you

- A system that classifies you in one of four seasons: spring, summer, fall and winter

- A system specific to an age group or that imposes any age limits

- A fashion system that suggests wearing certain clothing during only specific seasons of the year

- A system that only works for some women

Dressing Your Truth® is unlike any other fashion and beauty system out there. It is a system that honors the inner nature and personality of you, and the outer expression of your physical features. Once you know your distinct Type of beauty, *Dressing Your Truth®*

is a simple to learn formula that honors your own personal instinct and intuition of what looks best and feels best on you. There are five elements of *Dressing Your Truth*®. These five elements are expressed in clothing, jewelry, accessories, makeup color and application, and even your hair color, cut and style. Once you know your own Type of beauty, you will be ready to learn how to Dress Your Truth using the five elements as your guide. *Dressing Your Truth*® will give you the tools you need to take back your beauty.

Part 2

- THE FIRST STEP IN DRESSING YOUR TRUTH®: DISCOVER YOUR PERSONAL TYPE OF BEAUTY

- YOUR BEAUTY IS MORE THAN SKIN DEEP

- YOUR BEAUTY SIXTH SENSE

THE FIRST STEP IN DRESSING YOUR TRUTH®: DISCOVER YOUR PERSONAL TYPE OF BEAUTY

THIS IS WHERE THE FUN STARTS—discovering your personal Type of beauty. To help you in this discovery, I have adapted my more extensive *Energy Profiling®* system to fit the needs and purpose of this book.

My *Energy Profiling®* system is a groundbreaking and revolutionary personality profiling system that helps you discover your innate character and that of others. It is a study of movement, as it expresses itself through us in many facets of our lives. It is the natural expression of our human nature captured in: personality, behavior tendencies, thought and feeling processes, body language and physical features. With the help of the *Energy Profiling®* system, thousands of people have learned that their perceived weaknesses and flaws are actually their greatest strengths and gifts.

I have taken excerpts from my book *It's Just My Nature! A Guide to Knowing and Living Your True Nature* and adapted them to create my *Beauty Profile*SM system that is captured in this book. In *It's Just My Nature!* I offer a more thorough guide to using my *Energy Profiling®* system to help you more fully understand yourself and others. This *Beauty Profiling*SM system is an adaptation of the *Energy Profiling®* system, which has been refocused and reapplied here.

If you are a student of my *Energy Profiling®* information, you will no doubt see some similarities in this book. You will be surprised and delighted by new content that I have developed that is specific to women and their experience with their bodies that will help you identify your personal Type of beauty. I must stress it is *imperative* that you first discover your own Type of Beauty before you take the next step, the *Dressing Your Truth®* online course. *Dressing Your Truth®* only works in helping you bring out your beauty if you know what Type of woman you are. I feel confident that with the resources we have in place to assist you, you will know who you are and be very eager to live your truth and dress it.

Your Beauty is More Than Skin Deep

YOUR BEAUTY IS TRULY MORE THAN SKIN DEEP: it is actually created from the four elements in your DNA! These four elements create your inner beauty—your true nature, and your outer beauty—your physical features.

Think back to your chemistry class to recall what these four basic building blocks are. The four elements are nitrogen, oxygen, hydrogen and carbon. These elements create an innate movement that expresses itself naturally and effortlessly in every aspect of your life. Mother Nature truly is a beauty expert!

> MOTHER NATURE TRULY IS A BEAUTY EXPERT.

You might be asking, "What do the four elements have to do with me? And how in heaven's name do they relate to my beauty?" What you are about to discover may surprise you. These four elements, in terms of their natural movement and expression in you, have everything to do with your natural beauty.

The four elements are the basis of your Type of beauty. Your physical features, body language, personality, and many of your behavioral tendencies are influenced by the core expression of these four elements. These elements are connected to each of the four Types of beauty you will learn about in this book..

For simplicity, I have given each element a number and refer to each as a Type, for example:

- Nitrogen—Type 1
- Oxygen—Type 2

- Hydrogen—Type 3
- Carbon—Type 4

We have all four elements in us, but we lead with just one. I call this your Dominant Type. Our Dominant Type is the most prevailing expression influencing all aspects of our life. As I have previously mentioned, you will learn how this innate quality in each of us is influencing our looks, personality, and numerous behavior tendencies. Even when we try to override it and change our personality, this core movement cannot be silenced. We see it expressing itself most naturally when we are not thinking about it. It expresses itself in ways that we don't judge readily, like walking, talking, doodling and laughing, just to name a few examples.

I can determine a woman's Dominant Type most easily by simple assessments—that is, her demeanor when coming into a room of people she does not know, how she behaves during a class, how she moves through the process of learning new material, and the types of questions she asks, if she asks any. I can even tell by her facial features, the shape of her nose, the lines of her face, and the pitch and tone of her voice what Type she is.

> IT IS WHEN WE ARE NOT CONSCIOUSLY THINKING ABOUT WHO WE ARE THAT WHO WE TRULY ARE UNMISTAKABLY EXPRESSES ITSELF.

It is when we are not consciously thinking about who we are that who we truly are unmistakably expresses itself.

You express all four Types to varying degrees, including one dominant Type. I believe we are each unique in the creation and expression of who we are, yet I have found an uncanny similarity in the tendencies of expression found in women of the same Dominant Type. We are each unique and also very much the same within our Type.

The full model of *Energy Profiling*® that is taught in my book *It's Just My Nature!* is a simple, yet profound tool that helps us understand our natural gifts and talents, our strengths and weaknesses, our approach to the world, our ways of processing and perceiving our life experience and how we process information and make decisions. It helps us understand that we were created to express these core movements in every aspect of our lives, and to enjoy who we naturally are. With a deeper study of the *Energy Profiling®* model, you also more fully appreciate the character and natural expressions of others. Your judgments of other people drop away when you see them through the *Energy Profiling®* lens.

We teach women that all of the Types stand equal in their value, that there is not one more gifted or capable than another, not one more beautiful than another. When we are living in conscious alignment with our Dominant Type and our overall combination of all four Types, we experience a balanced life.

Every woman has the right and opportunity to be successful, ambitious, determined, fun, loving, caring, prosperous, generous, enlightened, and incredibly beautiful—all the qualities we strive for in our human experience. What will look different is the way we move and express ourselves in these qualities.

As you read through the description of each Type, open yourself up to who you really are. Pay attention to your heart more than your head. Your mind will tell you who you think you are, but your heart just knows it. Listen to your heart. It will not fail you.

RUTH'S STORY

Ruth's experience with a profiling class was life-changing for her. She was so excited to learn what Type she was because she instinctively knew that she was not living true to herself. As each Type was explained in the class, she realized that she was living in Type 4 energy, but it was not until the slide show was presented and she looked in the mirror that she saw that she was obviously a Type 1.

"I dutifully stood by the Type 1 picture," she says, "because that is what I looked like. I then read through the Type 1 word list and realized that is what I used to live until I got married 38 years ago. Over time I thought I had to be someone else to please my husband—it was not safe to be me. I now feel that I have been liberated!"

Ruth now knows that her Type 1 energy is her special gift, that there is nothing wrong with her! She has found her voice and is expressing her feelings and emotions more openly. How is her family reacting to this? Her four adult daughters are taking it all in and saying, "You go for it Mom—you look great and alive!" But her husband is saying, "You are not the person I married." It is obvious to Ruth that it will take some time for her husband to adjust to the real Ruth. But there is no turning back—she is empowered by knowing and living her truth!

Your Beauty Sixth Sense

EVERY WOMAN HAS A SIXTH SENSE FOR HER OWN BEAUTY. Very few women have developed this sixth sense because the fashion world only offers them one system, one that is based on styles and trends. For a woman to get in tune with her beauty sixth sense, she first needs to understand how her personality, body language and physical features influence what will look best on her. My *Beauty Profile*^{SM} system assessment is the first step in discovering your beauty sixth sense.

In order to know what looks best as an outer expression on you, you need to learn about what Type of woman you are. Since there are only four Types in my *Beauty Profiling*^{SM} system, you may wonder and even worry that *Dressing Your Truth*® is going to put you in a box, which would confine you to a certain look rather than freeing you to create your own personal style following your beauty sixth sense.

This is a fair concern. But before you prematurely conclude that four Types mean that there are only four looks in the *Dressing Your Truth*® world, consider the possibility that more is going on here. The truth is that, within each Type, there are countless varieties and variations that you can choose from in order to create a very unique look that will match your inner beauty and that will honor you. We actually find that most women feel that *Dressing Your Truth*® is incredibly liberating because they discover a personal sense of expertise and direction in what they shop for, rather than being at the mercy of trends.

I love the insight from Carolyn, a woman who recently started dressing her truth.

"I find that Carol's *Dressing Your Truth*® system provides the tools for any woman to honor her inner beauty. This system is great as it provides guidelines—not absolutes—for what works for your Type of beauty."

All women intuitively have a sixth sense of what will honor their natural beauty, but the fashion world has never offered a program that teaches you how to tap into this sixth sense and develop it. *Dressing Your Truth*® is a program that honors this sixth sense. Time and time again we hear from *Dressing Your Truth*® clients "Now I know why I have always loved that!" or "I used to trust my own instinct for beauty, then I started doubting myself and thought I had to do what was considered fashionable."

You have an instinct for what looks and feels best on your body, every woman does. My goal is to help women of all ages, colors, and sizes tap into to their own beauty sixth sense. Your beauty truly does start on the inside, and once you learn to dress your truth, you will have connected to the natural instinct you have to know what looks best on you because it feels right on you. The more you allow yourself to dress your truth, over time you will refine your beauty sixth sense and create a very personal look within the vast array of choices offered by *Dressing Your Truth*®.

Part 3

- THERE IS MORE THAN ONE TYPE OF WOMAN: WHAT TYPE ARE YOU?

- TYPE 1: THE BRIGHT, ANIMATED WOMAN

- TYPE 2: THE SUBTLE, SOFT WOMAN

- TYPE 3: THE RICH, DYNAMIC WOMAN

- TYPE 4: THE BOLD, STRIKING WOMAN

THERE IS MORE THAN ONE TYPE OF WOMAN: WHAT TYPE ARE YOU?

WHEN I WAS GROWING UP, the culture I was raised in depicted feminine nature as soft, gentle and sensitive. Not only were women soft and gentle, they were also more subdued, cute and perky. Men, on the other hand, in their masculine nature, were more aggressive and bold. We have been depicting women and men with these stereotypical qualities for centuries.

One of my biggest insights and discoveries in creating my *Beauty Profile*ᔆᴹ system is the discovery of the different Types of feminine.

> YOUR NEEDS NEVER GET MET BECAUSE YOU CONTINUE TO HIDE YOUR TRUE NATURE.

It is time to redefine the feminine!

The subtle, soft feminine alone can no longer be culturally acceptable or supportive to the different Types of women who are in the world.

At our Center for Living Your Truth in Draper, Utah, I have been involved in interventions with women who thought they were one Type of woman, only to discover they had lost touch with their true nature and had fooled themselves into believing they were a different Type of woman.

It is interesting to bring new light to a woman who is misperceiving her true identity! It is common that they are a bit confused and frustrated, and sometimes angry and afraid to see their true self.

How does this happen? How can a woman lose touch with her greatest qualities, her greatest strengths and gifts, her innately inborn beauty?

It happens every day in the lives of parents and children. When you are told that who you are is not okay when you are just naturally expressing yourself as a small child, you start to alter your personality to fit in and get your needs met. *The irony is, your needs never get met, because as you continue to hide your true nature, the love and acceptance you are seeking cannot be received by your true self.*

My Type 2 mom inadvertently sought ways to silence my determined, dynamic, Type 3 nature by shushing me frequently while I was in my childhood. I also witnessed the negative side of my nature via my Type 3 father who was powerfully reactive and intense—and unpredictably so—all through my years growing up. I did not want to be like either of them.

I am intrigued by female superstars who have stayed true to their feminine nature that was contrary to the stereotypical cookie-cutter feminine of the past. Pink, the rock artist professionally known as P!nk, is a great example of a young woman who refused to conform to becoming a subtle, soft feminine expression. Pink is a Type 4, a bold, striking feminine expression. She has lived true to it her entire life. She refused to be molded into a false expression of who she was when she launched her music career.

I recently watched Pink's biography on TV. This story is a perfect example of her staying true to her bold, blunt, Type 4 nature. In the process of being discovered as an upcoming musical artist, she had the opportunity to perform for a major recording label executive in his office. She was only 15 years old at the time. Half-way through the song she suddenly stopped and bluntly asked the question, "Are you going to stop shuffling through the papers on your desk and start listening to me?"

I believe the women who have lived true to their feminine expression are women who have risen to the top of their careers and pursuits, and we are intrigued by their confidence and honesty that naturally comes through in the roles they play. I have also noticed that women who are not living their truth can be unnecessarily critical of these successful women. They are unconsciously thinking, "Why does she get to live her truth? I conformed to the female standard. Why doesn't she have to?"

I recently read an article about the superstar comedian Joan Rivers. Joan is a Type 3—a rich, dynamic woman. Her nature is to be outspoken and edgy. She shared in this article that she had to go against what she thought was her feminine nature, the subtle, soft feminine stereotype of the time, to be a successful comedian. Ironically, Joan, if you are reading this, staying true to the Type of woman you are made all the difference in your years of success as a comedian.

In my *Beauty Profile*SM system, you will be introduced to four Types of feminine, each beautiful and remarkable, and each very much as feminine as the other, just expressed in different ways. Each is also incredibly sexy and powerful in their own right, and each fabulously beautiful when you know how to dress your truth.

The four Types of women that reflect the model I previously mentioned in this book, and that relate to the four elements we are all created from, are as follows:

- **Type 1: The Bright, Animated Woman**

- **Type 2: The Subtle, Soft Woman**

- **Type 3: The Rich, Dynamic, Woman**

- **Type 4: The Bold, Striking Woman**

You may see some of yourself in all four of the Types, yet you will find that you lead with one of the four and that you are definitely a dominant expression of one of the four.

You might be asking, "How can we reduce all women to just four classifications?" It is uncanny how consistently the movement of the four Types are expressed through women. I respect the fact that we are all created to be our own unique, expressive self. But I think you will agree with me after you have read the next few sections, that there is a remarkable similarity in the expressions of all of us that can be classified into four groups. Sure, within these groups you will find unique differences, but the general tendencies you will come to notice in aspects of our feminine expression are certainly there. It is important to remember that the tendencies being described and measured are very general and universal. Remember, this is all about your natural movement that expresses itself effortlessly in you.

DISCOVER YOUR TYPE

As you go through the *Beauty Profile*^{SM} process, you will see yourself in each Type—how the natural expression and movement of each Type influences your personality traits, behavior tendencies, thought and feeling processes, gifts and talents, personal space, body language, and most importantly, your physical features.

You have all four elements of nitrogen, oxygen, hydrogen, and carbon inherently in you. Every woman has a Dominant Type that does not change over her lifetime. When assessing yourself, you will be looking and feeling which of the four Types most aligns with you. I believe you innately know who you are and in your personal validation of that, you will take on a new level of ownership and permission to be yourself.

I will not offer you a personality assessment questionnaire in any of my Profiling resources. There is a higher percentage of error when we just look at personality and behavior (especially when only using a questionnaire), we have a safeguard for that in my *Beauty Profiling*^{SM} system that allows us to see more clearly what your true Type is: it is in the physical features.

We can assess how the movement of each Type expresses itself through your physical features. This provides a default mechanism for looking beyond personality and getting a more accurate reading of who you truly are. You likely have never looked at your nose and wondered if it resembles the shape of a circle, oval, rectangle or parallel lines. With my *Beauty Profile*^{SM} system, you will look at your nose in a whole new light!

Closely examining your physical features is valuable exercise for many women, helping them to discern their true Type. I tell women that their body never lies when it comes to telling the truth about who they are. After a woman has adapted and conformed herself to the needs of others throughout her life, she too often loses perspective about who she is. If you were shamed or disciplined for being your true self as a small child, you would be less likely to want to embrace your true nature due to some wounds that need to heal, and are very likely ready to heal now that you are reading this book. I believe you would not have come in contact with this material unless you were ready to heal!

MARCY'S NEIGHBOR'S STORY

Marcy (Type 1) shared this story about her neighbor who she invited to come to a Beauty Profile^{SM} class with her. Marcy had a marvelous experience learning her Type of beauty and seeing in her life where she was not honoring her true nature. She went on to attend a Dressing Your Truth®—The Ultimate Makeover event which took her experience to another level. She was so thrilled by how much this program had improved the quality of her life that she wanted her friend to experience this for herself. Her friend attended the class and when it came time for her to pick her Dominant Type, she went and stood in the Type 2 section.

As I usually do when I am teaching the class, I roamed around the room and shared feedback with anyone that did not appear to be in the right Type for them by what I was seeing in their Body Profile. When I came to her friend, I asked her, "What would be your next choice for your Type if this is not right for you?" She hesitated and replied, "Maybe a Type 1." I told her, "That is what I am seeing in your face. You have round cheeks, smiling eyes, and a turned up nose." I invited her to go stand in the Type 1 section and see how that felt. She agreed to do that, but later I noticed that she came back to the Type 2 group after only a little time had passed.

In our classes, we offer feedback based on our Body Profile assessment, and then let our clients find out their Type for themselves. Marcy's friend left that night trying to convince herself she was a Type 2. Marcy shared the rest of the story with me just recently. Her friend went home and that night had the worst night's sleep ever. She called Marcy and shared how confused she was. The next night she was restless again, and, finally fed up and frustrated, took her Type 2 watch off, threw it across the room and yelled, "I am not a 2. I am a 1!"

The information at the Profiling class spoke to her at a deep, innate level that she could not deny. She wrestled with it in her mind and discovered that she had been unnecessarily fighting with her identity for many years. She is now happily living in her true nature, and living life with more zest and bounce, which is totally true to her Type 1 nature!

My Beauty Profiling^SM *system truly is more of a right brain, intuitive personal experience. When we are operating more from heart than logic, we have a much better sense of who we are. When logic is our reference to who we are, we often get confused, conflicted, and question our innate nature. Remember to trust your heart, your feelings about who you truly are!*

ASPECTS OF FEMININE NATURE

I have consistently found that the natural expression and movement of each of the four Types appears in many aspects of our human experience. What we will look at in this book is where and how the natural expression and movement of each of the four Types is being expressed in the following aspects of our feminine nature.

GIFTS AND TALENTS—The natural movement of our Dominant Type supports us in having a unique gift and talent that not only adds great value to our own life, but also contributes to the wholeness of humanity working in harmony. What is ironic is that, quite often, we judge the very gift nature has endowed us with to be a weakness and a flaw. Knowing your natural gifts and talents that are supported by your Dominant Type will be amazingly supportive and freeing to you.

PERSONALITY TRAITS—Even though we can consciously manipulate our personal-

> YOU ARE ALWAYS EXPERIENCING YOU.

ity to play roles and hide our true nature in these roles, we still see the expressions of each Type pushing through all of these roles, insisting on being expressed naturally. These natural expressions cannot be totally silenced, but they can be restrained, shamed, judged and deemed unacceptable. Most likely, what you have disliked about yourself or judged as unacceptable could be your natural self and who you truly are. This is one of the most important concepts of both Energy and *Beauty Profiling*SM systems.

THOUGHT AND FEELING PROCESSES—The four Types are the most expressive in our inner world of thoughts and feelings. The inner world creates the outer world—it all begins with our own inner thoughts and feelings. This is our personal space that we can never step outside of. You are always experiencing you. Everything in your outer world is a reflection of your inner world. How you perceive your reality is being influenced by your Dominant Type, and

47

your Dominant Type is influencing what you value in yourself and others.

BEHAVIORAL TENDENCIES—These include how we express the natural movement of the four Types in our communication, personal relationships, social interaction, work, physical activity, and the management of money and even our shopping tendencies and perceptions of our body and physical appearance.

DOODLING—Doodling is an innate activity that demonstrates the natural movement of who you really are without conscious judgment. Just pause for a moment and think about how you doodle. Look in the next sections to find which Dominant Type captures your doodle. It's not 100 percent accurate 100 percent of the time, but it's very close. It was correct for me!

BODY LANGUAGE—We will also look at how the movement of the four Types is expressed in the way you walk, sit, stand, talk, use your hands, what your word choices are, and how you maintain your personal space, including what interior design elements you are drawn to.

PHYSICAL FEATURES—The physical body is a manifestation of your inner essence. The vibration and movement of the four Types are expressed and shaped in all your physical features. Most people are blended, showing lines and shapes of at least two of the Types, but you do have a predominant expression that honors one of the four. The body—and the energy in it—does not lie! It is honestly expressing your true feminine nature.

HOW YOUR ENERGY AFFECTS OTHER PEOPLE—As you live and express yourself, your leading Type will shine through, and will have an effect on other people. Understanding this can help you identify what characteristics will either inspire or irritate other Types.

HOW YOUR APPEARANCE AFFECTS OTHER PEOPLE—Your appearance has an effect on other people. A common mistake is to dress in a way that attempts to hide what we think is a weakness but which is really our strength. People will misjudge us according to how we dress. It is important that we dress according to our Type, so our outward appearance is in alignment with who we really are.

MOST COMMON FASHION MISTAKES—I'll go over the common fashion mistakes that each Type makes—where each Type stumbles—and how you can overcome these mistakes.

SHOPPING TENDENCIES—You may not realize it, but you have unique shopping tendencies. I'm talking about clothes shopping, not shopping for groceries. Some move through a store quickly, others take their time. Some benefit from taking a friend along while others do better shopping alone. Some of your tendencies are strengths while others hinder your shopping experience.

BEAUTY CODE WORD—Each Type has a beauty code word. The word captures the each Type's natural expression of beauty in a single word.

YOUR BEAUTY SIXTH SENSE— You have an innate beauty sixth sense of what looks good and feels right on your body. You were born with this intuitive gift as a woman. *Dressing Your Truth*® will help you discover and, for many, rediscover, this often hidden gift that the fashion world ignores. Each Type of woman has a sixth sense of her own beauty.

FAMOUS WOMEN OF A TYPE—For each Type, you'll see a list of famous women who are of that given Type. It will help you understand your Type more when you see it displayed in popular, well-known women.

As I mentioned a few paragraphs ago, you may see yourself in each Type. That is because you have all four Types in you. You are created from the four primary elements that influence the movement of each Type. That is what makes you a whole woman. But you are dominant in one of the four Types. I have not met one woman yet that isn't. Your secondary Type of beauty does play a strong supporting role for most women when it comes to learning how to dress your truth.

Not every woman exhibits the same level of movement within each Dominant Type. There are levels within each Dominant Type. There are some women that have stronger expressions of their Dominant Type's movement and are what I would call a textbook, classic example of their Type's tendencies.

HEDY'S STORY

Before she took my Beauty Profile[SM] *course, Hedy was a reserved, quiet woman who took a lot of criticism and bad treatment from everybody because she was afraid to speak out. She grew up in a family with a great rift between her mother and father's side. Her father's mother and aunt also lived with her family. There were two factions. Hedy and her younger brother Hein belonged to their mother's side or faction, and her youngest brother Norbert belonged to her father's side, especially to her grandmother.*

She was a cheerful child and often danced around and sang with joy. But this was not acceptable to her father's faction, and the joy was literally beaten out of her. When Hedy's mother died after a four-year struggle with ALS, the light went out from her. She was only 14. She had to cover up her joyful nature in order to survive in her father's faction.

"This is how I then became oblivious to my true inner nature," Hedy says.

When Hedy did my Profiling course, she found out that she was a Type 1. No way, she thought. However, the more she considered it during the ensuing weeks, the more she realized that she really was a Type 1. "I remembered who I truly was," she says. "I remembered the light and joy within me."

As time has passed, the light within her has grown stronger, as well as the joy. Hedy says that the impact of the Beauty Profile^{SM} process has been so profound that it has changed her life. She is now more aware of her inner nature and does not tolerate bad treatment from others anymore. Her relationship with her 18-year-old son has also changed for the better. The discord is gone. Now there is harmony, and a lot more fun! Her friends have noticed the difference, too, as she is far more upbeat than before.

Please understand that in each of us are variable levels of our Dominant Type. Just notice what your tendencies are and what Type you see yourself as. As time passes, you will find that you can more readily assess your natural expressions and movements, and most of all, you learn to follow your heart. In the end, your heart and intuition will not lead you astray.

There is no wrong way to find your true, feminine nature. Your path will be perfect for you though it may not always seem so. Ultimately, after some experimentation, it all works itself out perfectly.

We have had clients who at first thought they were a certain Type, but then after learning what their physical features were saying about who they are, they came to realize they had been repressing their true nature or misjudging it.

It is possible that you had to hide your true nature in your childhood due to feeling unsafe or unacknowledged. Even though this might be the case, you will recognize the natural movement of your core true self in the following sections.

I believe women innately know who they are if they will tune in and honor their true, core nature that expressed itself so freely in the earliest childhood days. You might even want to look back to those days and notice what your movement was like as a child. Were you buoyant and bouncy, calm and serene, assertive and determined, or could you play well by yourself and sit still readily?

As a brief recap, here are the three primary areas to look at to find your true feminine nature:

1. Your inner expression. This includes your thoughts and feelings, perceptions and values.

2. Your outer expression. This includes your gifts and talents, your personality traits, your body language and behavior tendencies.

3. The mirror. This includes your physical features and movement of your bodylines.

The majority of what you read in the section on your Dominant Type will speak to you. The levels at which we express our Dominant Type will vary from person to person, and we must take into account the influence of our secondary energies. Together, the unique composition of all four Types within you produces your very individual beauty. Not everyone will match any given Type 100 percent, but many will!

Ironically, consider the possibility that you have deemed your greatest gifts your biggest weaknesses and your natural beauty in your physical features as flaws. It is not uncommon that after a woman has finished the *Beauty Profile*^{SM} course that she has one of the biggest ah-ha moments of her life! They realize that their innate gifts and talents that are being influenced by their Dominant Type are really tremendous blessings.

However, all along they have been perceiving these qualities as flaws in their character.

What a relief! You no longer have to try to quiet and stop your God-given feminine nature!

I recently expressed to my daughter Jenny (Type 1) that I have come to realize that, as a Type 3, my energy moves forward swiftly, pushing things and people to create outcomes. Yes, I can be experienced as forceful and intense at times, but the more consciously I manage my natural movement in balance with the other three Types, I allow others to experience my gifts in a balanced way.

I have realized that trying to stop or slow my natural movement would be as easy as stopping Niagara Falls! In fact, I use the following metaphor any time I start to judge my natural qualities in a negative manner, comparing it to standing on the banks of the Niagara River and saying: "Knock it off, Niagara Falls. You're just way too pushy. Can't you just calm down and be more like the Mississippi River?"

Read each section on the four Types of women and see yourself in the one you have the most connection with. Have fun with this, enjoy yourself, and notice when you begin to put judgments and labels on what you are learning about. After all, it is all just natural expression and movement supporting us in expressing who we truly are as women.

Remember that every woman has the right and opportunity to be successful, prosperous, happy, fulfilled, creative, and generous, in all the qualities we strive for in our feminine experience. It is our Dominant Type that makes us different in the way we move and express our true feminine nature in pursuit of these ambitions.

Type 1: The Bright, Animated Woman

Primary Movement: *Upward, Light*
Natural Gift: *Ideas—"I have a new idea, and we can do it!"*
Dominant Quality: *Cheerfully lifting us up to feel more fun and hope.*
Beauty Code Word: *Cute!*

THE TYPE 1 EXPRESSION COMES FROM THE ELEMENT OF NITROGEN/AIR, and its natural primary movement is upward and light. If you have a dominant Type 1 movement, you have an upward, light energy. You are naturally inspiring, fun-loving and hopeful. Your dominant shapes in physical features are animated shapes, like a circle, heart, and the points of a star. This is visible in the eyes, the cheeks, and the overall body and facial shape.

Type 1 energy is an extrovert expression moving upward and out to create in this world. You have the highest level of natural movement of all the Types. This natural, high-level, upward, light, buoyant, random movement can be consistently observed through all aspects of your feminine experience.

Other key words that describe the movement of this energy in a dominant Type 1 woman are: fresh, youthful, animated, bubbly, brilliant, radiant, connected then disconnected, crisp, fun and unstructured.

Due to the high movement that expresses itself spontaneously, you may have been told a lot as a child—and even in your adult life—to "Settle down!" or "Stop moving."

Your energy is like the sun shining brightly or a burst of fresh blossoms on a cherry tree. You truly are a breath of fresh air, just like your dominant element—nitrogen/air!

Keeping life light and fun is one of the primary motives for a Type 1 woman. Most cultures have labeled this movement as a childlike expression and only acceptable when we are at a party, taking a break or on vacation. We have perceived it as a movement that we should grow out of when we become adults, and that to be successful, we have to move through life more seriously.

This is not true.

Type 1 energy is always light, fresh, and fun, no matter the age of the woman. In fact, it is critical that a Type 1 woman come up with a way of approaching the activities of her life (whether it be work or play) in a manner that makes them more fun and light.

My daughter Jenny (Type 1) has found many ways to add this element of fun to her day-to-day life experience. She realized using a paper Day-Timer or electronic handheld PDA was not fun for her. To organize her life, each week she takes a piece of paper and draws up her weekly calendar with all her commitments on it, and fills the paper with animated pictures, which she then puts on the refrigerator. She shared with me, "Having the animated doodles and pictures helps me feel like what I have to do can be fun and light."

MARCY'S STORY

When Marcy first heard about my Beauty Profiling^{SM} system, she was curious to know more but was not really that enthused. She assumed it was like other personality tests she had taken over the years that attempt to classify people by everything from colors to seasons to star signs and alphabet soup. She was very surprised to find that my Beauty Profile℠ course really isn't like any other program.

Once Marcy discovered and accepted the fact that her leading Type is a 1 (and she admits she came kicking and screaming to that conclusion!), she was able to see very clearly how the strengths and weaknesses of her 1-ness played out in her life. She now knows why she loves starting projects but not finishing them, and she has a much better sense of which complementary Types can help her be more effective in managing her business and life in general.

One of the first things Marcy did after being profiled was call her business partner—who she is quite sure is a dominant Type 4—and laughingly acknowledge that she must drive her crazy sometimes, and now she knows why!

"I have seen many relationship revelations come about in my family as my children have been profiled," Marcy says. "The result is always positive and leads to a great deal of acceptance and understanding—of each other and of us."

NATURAL GIFTS AND TALENTS

Type 1s initiate the cycle of wholeness by coming up with new ideas and the inspiration and the hope of making them come true. Animation creates new life, and Type 1 energy creates new life.

If you were to put this into a phrase, the Type 1 phrase would be, **"I have a new idea, and we can do it."**

You truly do believe in the possibility of all your ideas. You can expect that you will produce more ideas than you will ever be able to accomplish. At the time the idea or impulse of a new possibility comes to you, you believe in it at the same moment it hits you. You readily express your ideas in a way that enables you to see others believing in them and the idea. Because you always have more ideas than can be executed—and you will naturally become distracted by other new ideas as they pop up—it can confuse and frustrate other people when it appears to them that you have dropped the ball.

Type 1 women move through life like a bouncing ball. They take the ball and run with it, and they can also drop some balls along the way since they create too many new balls to juggle. Your primary shape is a circle, the shape of a ball. You can see the bounce of the ball in your movement from point A to point B. Like Type 1 energy, a ball can bounce off its surface from any possible angle, in any possible direction! One of the dominant shapes in Type 1 facial features is a circle or the shape of a ball.

You are naturally optimistic, and you look at everything from the bright side. You are like the sun, shining brightly on humanity, with a bright, brilliant nature or disposition. The shape of the sun is also a circle. Of any Type, you are the most able to overlook difficulties and believe in the possibility of success. If you fail, you do not worry about it for long, but console yourself easily and move on.

Ideas come easily and readily to you. Your natural movement of being light and carefree can keep you from following through and finishing things. Your constant challenge is execution and bringing plans to the final outcome. My daughter Jenny (Type 1) shares, "I have great, big ideas, some of them elaborate ideas, but I know I

YOU ARE LIKE THE SUN, SHINING BRIGHTLY ON HUMANITY.

benefit from getting help to make it all work, to make a plan and to execute the big ideas."

You are keenly alive in your environment, and of all the Types, you are the most able to experience the present moment of your life.

Important: It is important that a Type 1 have fun and keep things light. If you try and slow down your movement and move more deliberately through life, you will just be going through the motions, having lost your connection with your core true nature. You will be out of balance from your upward, light energy if you try to create too much structure or try to slow down and be too deliberate.

The same natural tendencies that are your gift and talents can also be a challenge in your life, causing imbalance and disharmony. When your dominant movement is taking over your life and is not balanced by the other three Types that are also a part of your being, it can be a challenge being you!

Challenge: You can get stuck in the idea phase, bringing in more ideas than you can follow through with. You easily disconnect from one thing that is already in progress to start something new. You like the feeling of newness so you leave other things undone that have already been started.

Challenge: Because new ideas, events and people distract you easily, you have a tendency to not always follow through. Others may experience you as false, unbelievable, and not to be taken seriously.

I recently told my Type 1 daughter, "You need to allow for your randomness within a world that demands a certain amount of structure, and you need to follow-through on things that support your relationships and quality of life. Be more conscious of where you drop the ball, so it does not interfere with the harmony you desire in your relationships."

Challenge: Because you are so light, you have a tendency to make light of things that are hurting you at a deep level. You may shy away from standing up for yourself, and speaking what is true for you when others feel differently. You may hold back and adapt to others continually, and in this, lose yourself. This will cause your light to dim over time, and you will not know who you are as you continue to play roles that are not the true you.

PERSONALITY TRAITS

You like change and new experiences. You talk readily and easily to people. You like to keep things light and fun, encouraging and motivating others along the way. If someone is feeling down, you will readily encourage them, cheerleading them to feel better. You move forward with excited and hopeful determination, always making it fun along the way.

You are naturally cheerful and have an innate love of pleasure and fun. You do not like to be alone. You love company and amusement, and you want to enjoy life. You tend to have an elated spirit, you are not given to worry and anxiety, and your nature is to be carefree. You are consistent in not being consistent—changing plans and living your life with abandon, not structure. You are able to respond to changing situations spontaneously with an inspired perspective.

The dominant element that expresses itself in you is nitrogen/air. Phrases commonly used to describe your personality are: "You are a breath of fresh air," or when it becomes a judgment, "You are such an airhead."

Many things which cause other Types a great deal of anxiety and trouble do not affect a Type 1, because you are an optimist and, as such, overlook difficulties and prefer to look at all of life from the sunny side. Even when you are exasperated and sad, you soon find your balance again. Your sadness does not last long, and gives way quickly to happiness. This sunny quality allows you to get along well with others, even with persons generally difficult to work with.

You are friendly in speech and behavior and can pleasantly entertain others by interesting narratives and witticisms.

Challenge: When you have not followed through or have let someone down by not keeping your commitments and not communicating, you have a tendency to give yourself excuses and make up stories as to why you could not follow through. If a new point of view presents itself, this may readily upset your plans, which you have made previously. This inconsistency often causes people to think that the Type 1 woman is flaky. You deny such judgments because, in your mind, there is a good reason for your change of direction. You forget that at times it would be supportive to your relationships to consider other people's feelings and to look into and investigate the ramifications of change before you start to make it. As you are aware that you are easily captivated by every new idea or mood, you need to more consciously manage what you have already committed yourself to with other people.

Challenge: Before you have mastered one subject, your interest wanes because new impressions have already captured your attention. You love light work, which attracts your attention, where there is no need of deep thought or great effort. You can be hard to convince that you may tend to be superficial about things—on the contrary, you imagine that you have grasped a subject wholly and perfectly. You are so good at convincing others, you convince yourself. The evidence will be seen in areas like school where grades are applied or jobs that require more structure, and any other aspects of life that have standards of measurement you have to apply to them.

Challenge: In your enjoyment, you can be very frivolous. You can be inconsistent at work or entertainment—you love variety in everything, like a hummingbird that flies from flower to flower, the child who soon tires of the new toy, or the woman who grows weary of a new outfit.

Challenge: Because you are so adaptable with your light, non-structured, airy energy, and you have a sunny nature that boosts others up, you have a tendency to consider what others want before you consider what you want. With this tendency of saying "What do you want?" to others, you may also be trying to avoid taking responsibility in case things don't work out. This may even develop into feeling like you need to ask for permission for anything you want. If this is happening to you, you have allowed your upward, light, airy energy to take over, losing yourself in your own carefree nature.

THOUGHT AND FEELING PROCESSES

Your thoughts and feelings are quick and spontaneous. You process information so quickly that others can perceive you as not thinking things through. You know quickly what is right for you. Follow your quick intuition and impulses to stay balanced in your life.

Because Type 1s think things through quickly, they can appear to others to not take things seriously. To the rest of us it appears you would need to take more time to think it through, but with the radiant, light, brilliant movement you are supported with, you do not. It is common for Type 1s to feel they have to slow their energy down and change who they are to be taken seriously by others.

If you are a Type 1, you organize things quickly in your mind, but you may look disorganized to others. This is because both your movement and your approach to life is more random. You can juggle many things at once, so it all fits together for you. Because you have quick mental organization, you are highly intuitive and can sense possibilities that others cannot.

Challenge: Because you readily see what doesn't exist physically and express your belief in it, you can attract disbelief from others, which can cause you to doubt your own inspiration.

Challenge: Your high level of belief can cause you to be gullible and appear naïve to others. As you recognize your tendencies and honor your true nature, most of this will drop off in your life and you will be seen as ingenious!

While walking on the beach on a recent trip to Hawaii to visit our family home there, my daughter Jenny was lamenting over her own personal struggle of being a dominant Type 1 energy. She was not allowing herself to be who she is and this trip was providing a lot of reminders of how she was not. She was getting headaches on a daily basis the first few days we were there. She realized her headaches were an indicator to her that she was trying to conform to be someone she was not.

She was judging her light, airy ways as weak and immature. She was even bothered by the sun coming out every day and shining brightly on us! She made me laugh when she shared, "Mom, I was even mad at the sun for being so bright and shiny. It just kept reminding me that I was not living true to myself, thinking I need to be more serious and deliberate in my approach to life." She jokingly started shaking her fist at the sun, saying, "How dare you be so bright and warm. You better just knock it off sun. You are really starting to get to me!"

Jenny once again committed to be herself—her Type 1 animated, fresh, light self. At the end of our walk, she had an impulse of an idea to run into the ocean with all her clothes on and just go for a swim right then and there. She told me before she took off, "I need to follow this impulse just to honor myself right now." It was a lot of fun to watch her skip off into the water!

COMMUNICATION

You value change, fun, and spontaneity in your communication. You love having fun while understanding and connecting with others. Type 1 women are the chatters and talkers of the four Types.

You like to talk, chitchat, and enjoy verbal interaction while doing other things. You can often interrupt or jump from topic to topic in midair when you are in the middle of a conversation because you process information so much faster than other people do. You speak what you are thinking almost instantly. You feel no need to sort it out before you spit it out! You are frank, talkative, social, and your emotions are readily expressed.

You relish good conversation, but can also go with the flow. You can chitchat or make small talk with the best of them. In your conversations, you can move from one idea to another so quickly, it appears random to others. You like to change focus often and move from one thing to the next, taking a lot in. You have a high level of belief and like to share that and use it to encourage others.

Challenge: You can appear random and ungrounded to others, since you can change your mind effortlessly and agree with others easily. Therefore, you have an opportunity to learn how to say what is true for you, be true to your intuition and inspiration, and stay in your own light, upward momentum without feeling either guilty or pushy about it. Speak your truth as quickly as you know it. Act on your first impulse and trust it.

BEHAVIORAL TENDENCIES

You move like a babbling brook, bubbling along buoyantly in rapid succession, turning from one activity to another.

RELATIONSHIPS—You seek a wide and broad range of friendships. You are not selective or exclusive. You are not insistent upon acceptance of your ideas or plans. You agree readily with others' wishes, being compliant and adaptable.

Challenge: You are so adaptable you may lose yourself to others. You are especially vulnerable to losing yourself as you adapt to Type 3s and 4s.

SOCIAL—You have an eagerness to participate with others, whether at work or play. To you there is no difference between work and play if it is light and fun and you can be sociable with others. You readily make acquaintances with other people. You are very communicative, loquacious, and associate easily with strangers. At social gatherings, the best part for you is bouncing from room to room and person to person.

TIMELINESS—You have a tendency for being late. You are consistent in your lateness. If you get close to the agreed upon time to be somewhere, getting there close to the time feels like being on time to you. You tend to be late because of your nature of being distracted as you move from point A to point B.

WORK—You excel in positions that require innovation, new ideas, intuition, creativity, fun, and a sense of freedom. You can concentrate on multiple tasks at one time, but remember you tend to leave tasks unfinished because you love the freshness of starting something new. The more you are aware of this tendency the more you can manage your natural movement to be a gift in your life rather than a detriment, especially if you can delegate the completion of tasks to others.

MONEY—You tend to be very carefree with your money. Because you are not deeply attached to anything, including money, you can see a lot of money come and go in your life. You are a generous person and because you love to light up someone's life, you easily share your money and goods with others to bring a smile to their face. You enjoy using your money in this way.

PHYSICAL ACTIVITY—You prefer group activities, whether work or play, and are not easily satisfied with individual projects unless the project you are working on is motivated by doing something for someone else. My daughter Jenny (Type 1) told me she is extremely motivated to finish things that she is doing for other people because she loves to see the smile on their faces when she shares it with them. When you are exercising, you prefer to socialize at the same time and prefer group sports to individual sports.

BODY LANGUAGE

Not all of your body language and physical features will express themselves in a Type 1 movement. Most women are blended in their physical features, so you won't see yourself in all these expressions, but you will notice many expressions of body language and physical features that are Type 1 if you are a dominant Type 1 women.

WALKING—You walk with a buoyant, bouncy spring in your step.

SITTING/STANDING—You sit and stand with a lot of movement, shifting your position often. You can appear to be restless and fidgety to others, as you do not like to sit or stand still, focusing on one thing for very long. You often sit with your legs crossed, what we call Indian style, or very comfortably on the floor.

VOICE/LANGUAGE—A Type 1 voice is a higher pitch and can even sound squeaky. It is an animated voice, or like a child's. When you answer the phone, even though you are an adult, people may say, "Can I talk to your mother?" If that is the case, you have a Type 1 voice!

Due to your bubbly, buoyant nature, when you speak, the tone of your voice rises and falls a lot. You speak with more dramatic, expressive, descriptive, animated language, and a lot of laughter.

You always talk with your hands—actually, your whole body will be involved in expressing what you are saying. You like to use animated words and descriptions. Rachael Ray, a popular American TV show host, is a perfect example of Type 1 language. She does a lot of cooking on her show and she uses animated words like *delish* or *yum-o*, and uses acronyms like *EVOO* for Extra Virgin Olive Oil, and calls a sandwich a *sammie* all through her show. My Type 1 friend Lori will end her phone conversation with me using expressions like "See you later, Toots!" It doesn't bother me when she says it because of her animated nature; but if I were to say it, it would sound out of character!

Giggling is common for a Type 1 woman, but you may not notice your tendency for giggling throughout the day or when you are talking to someone. Something else you may do that you have not noticed is using the phrase, "Just kidding!" frequently. My daughter Jenny (Type 1) says this immediately after she has teased someone or said something lightly sarcastic.

DOODLING—You doodle using shapes that represent your natural movement—circles, stars and hearts—with repetition that creates a feeling of animation, youthfulness and liveliness.

PERSONAL SPACE—You like to keep things in sight, out and around. You can be messy and appear disorganized to others. You would really rather not have to take the time to clean up. You figure you can do it later, or just do it real quick, so you can go do something more fun. If you create ways to make cleaning fun, it is more interesting to you.

Due to your very quick and spontaneous thought process, you have a tendency to misplace things, car keys being one of the most common items. You also frequently lose track of glasses, wallets and purses. You are already on to your next thought, and will not pay attention to where you put your keys. Jenny knows her tendency for this pattern and now consciously puts her keys in the same place or even has a few back up sets to cover herself when she doesn't remember to put the keys in the designated place.

When you travel, it can be a challenge to narrow down your clothing choices, so you tend to bring a lot of clothes on your trip to give yourself plenty of options.

INTERIOR DESIGN—You like a lot of decorations. You have the highest movement in your being of any of the types, so seeing that high level of movement in your physical surroundings is very comfortable to you. You like things out where you can see them. You have a lot of fun with decorating for holidays, especially Halloween! It is common that it is your favorite holiday. Everything about Halloween screams Type 1—the dressing up, the trick or treat theme, the candy, the spoofing—all are animated and fun.

PHYSICAL FEATURES

The overall quality of your physical expression is animated, youthful and cute. Your bone structure creates circles and points of a star with your features being asymmetrical or random. For visual examples and pictures of Type 1 facial features, please watch the *Beauty Profile*^{SM} course at *www.dressingyourtruth.com*.

SKIN AND SKIN TEXTURE—Type 1 skin is fresh and youthful. Freckles, small moles randomly on the skin, blemishes and reddening (blushing) of the skin are all Type 1 skin features.

FACE SHAPE—Circular or heart shaped.

CHEEKS—Circles, what we call apple cheeks. Dimples are also a Type 1 feature.

NOSE—A circle shape on the tip of the nose or what we call a button nose. Also, a point of a star which can been seen on the tip of your nose. Meryl Streep has a point of a star nose. Type 1 energy moves upward, so a turned up nose is a Type 1 nose. A Type 1 nose also tends to be smaller in size.

EYEBROWS—Come to a point right over the eye, or are half circles.

EYES—Round, pop out, with a sparkle or light in the eyes. A unique Type 1 feature is what we call smiling eyes. When a Type 1 woman smiles, her whole face smiles with an upward, light movement. Even your eyes and the lines on the sides of your eyes are moving upward when you smile.

HANDS— Cherub looking, chubby fingers, with a small, youthful appearance. You also have short fingers, short nail beds and nails that can be circular or turn upward.

HOW YOUR ENERGY AFFECTS OTHER PEOPLE

Your energy creates an ambience of youthfulness and fun. Your upward, light energy lifts people around you. You are naturally a light to the rest of us. At times, your high level of movement can get annoying and feel intrusive to other Types, especially a dominant Type 4. One of our *Dressing Your Truth®* clients who is a dominant Type 1 shared, "As a business owner, I have the opportunity to deal with a lot of different people. Now I know why I annoyed some people and they did not take me seriously in my role. I am especially aware when I am dealing with a Type 4 person to tone my 1-ness down a bit and respect their needs. This has allowed me to create some fabulous business opportunities that I may not have been able to create if I had come off too random and playful."

As you are conscious of your natural movement and are more aware of who you are interacting with, you will be able to manage yourself in a way that supports others in being in rapport with you. As you stay conscious of who you are and love who you are, rather

69

than judge your natural movement and try to silence it, you will be consistently aligned with your core true nature and others will always enjoy being around you.

Now I'll explore some specifics around fashion and a Type 1 woman.

SENDING THE RIGHT MESSAGE: HOW YOUR APPEARANCE AFFECTS OTHER PEOPLE

When you are not dressing your truth, you send a message that conflicts with who you truly are. Your nature is to be bright and animated, and when you wear clothes that make you appear either more serious or subdued, your true nature is disguised to most others, and you can often be judged as silly and annoying. Type 1 women often think, "If I dress more bright and colorful, I will come across as too animated." This is not the case. When you dress your truth, your inner truth is in harmony with your outer appearance, and you will be taken seriously for who you are: a bright, animated woman.

Even in a professional setting where you want to be taken seriously, putting on a serious look is not in your best interest. When you learn to dress your truth, you learn you can still look incredibly professional and maintain your brilliance and shine. (We actually have a special course in our *Dressing Your Truth*® online course that is entitled, "How to Dress Your Professional Truth.")

What you are wearing sends a message to other people which influences their first impression of you. You may be judged in a negative light because your true nature is not being honored by your appearance. You have a gift of bringing light and hope to any situation. Set the mood everywhere you go by dressing your truth and letting your light shine through your outer appearance.

MOST COMMON FASHION MISTAKES

It is common for a Type 1 woman to have a tendency to wear a lot of black in an effort to be taken more seriously and not look so youthful and cute. Ironically, it only conflicts with her light, fresh nature, making her natural animated expression more pronounced and amplified, which then comes across as silly!

Sarah Palin gave us a good example of this when she was running for the Vice-Presidency of the United States in 2008. Sarah is a dominant Type 1 who was dressing like a Type 4, wearing more bold, structured, stylized black clothing. Even her eyeglasses were heavy and structured. When a woman appears to the world in these styles, we expect a bold, concise expression from her. When Sarah would wink at the camera and speak in her animated, playful tone, she appeared silly and ridiculous, which the media picked up and then used to attempt to make a fool out of her. If she had hoped she would be taken more seriously by dressing the way she did, it only backfired, which hurt her reputation. If Sarah had been dressing her truth, who knows, maybe it could have swung the results of the presidential race that year!

I recently met a Type 1 woman who obviously had straightened her curly hair. I asked her why she was straightening her hair and she replied, "I think women are taken more seriously when they have straight hair!" Wow, who came up with that misconception? I told her she would always look her best bringing out the natural movement of her hair. I shared with her as she expressed her true nature as a Type 1 woman, she would be taken seriously for just *who she is*, a fun-loving brilliant woman!

SHOPPING TENDENCIES

Because you love new possibilities and a lot of options, you can get overwhelmed with all the fashion options that are available these days. In a fashion world where pretty much anything goes, you may have experimented with multiple hair colors and styles, having great fun changing your appearance. You have a tendency to become overwhelmed in a store when you have to consider so many possibilities. What motivates you to make a purchase is you think what you are buying would be fun to wear! Or a new hairstyle would be fun! You probably have a lot of different looks and styles hanging in your closet but not a strong sense of what is right for you. Due to so many possibilities you often just buy what is on sale or on the mannequins!

You prefer *not* to shop alone. You love to interact with others in anything you do, so shopping is more fun when it is also a social event for you. You might find that if you are having so much fun socializing, you are not paying close attention to what you are buying, and when you get home, you wonder why you bought some of the items you did!

My daughter Jenny (Type 1) is grateful to know how to dress her truth. She shares, "I used to get so overwhelmed with all the possibilities and it would take so long to find something I loved. I ended up buying a lot of things I didn't love and didn't feel great in. Now that I know how to dress my truth, it is easy—I go in and know which possibilities to completely ignore and focus on the ones that are perfect for me. I love it!"

THE TYPE 1 WOMAN BEAUTY CODE WORD

Every woman is remarkably beautiful, no matter what Type she is. Your natural feminine expression enables you to have a certain kind of beauty that radiates the Type of woman you are. When *Dressing Your Truth*® and honoring your truest beauty, a Type 1 woman will be told a lot, "You are so cute!" *Cute* is the beauty code word for Type 1 women.

I have heard Type 1 women complaining that they don't want to look cute or be called cute. These are women who are still judging their light airy nature to be inadequate and superficial. When you know the true power of your feminine self, you embrace and welcome the words that depict your true feminine nature and your true beauty. When someone calls you cute, in your heart, you know it means, "You are a brilliant, fun-loving, amazing and beautiful woman!"

Looking cute and youthful when you are 65 is a good thing. You never have to grow old. Embrace this.

YOUR BEAUTY SIXTH SENSE DRESSING YOUR TRUTH TIP

Because you naturally have a light and buoyant nature, it is important that what you wear on your body feels light and free to you. If it feels heavy and cumbersome to you, it is going against your beauty sixth sense. Just ask yourself these questions when you are trying something on, "Does this feel light on my body?" and "Do I feel free in it?" If you can say yes, you are honoring your beauty sixth sense.

FAMOUS TYPE 1 WOMEN

Paula Abdul, Drew Barrymore, Christie Brinkley, Katie Couric, Doris Day, Ellen Degeneres, Sally Field, Goldie Hawn, Katie Holmes, Vanessa Hudgens, Gladys Knight, Marilyn Monroe, Sarah Palin, Dolly Parton, Rachael Ray, Sherri Shepherd, Meryl Streep, Raven Symone, Shirley Temple, and Reese Witherspoon.

APRIL'S STORY

Here is story about April, a Type 1 woman, told in her own words:

"After reading your book and attending a profiling class, I thought I must be a Type 2 who couldn't sit still for long, or possibly a Type 3 who just needed to try harder —no way was I a Type 1!

I didn't even consider it until I was draped and saw for myself that the Type 1 fabrics and metals looked the best on me. Talk about a paradigm shift!

"I had spent my entire life thinking I should be a 2 or a 3, and now I realize why I was making life so hard. I had to get right to the core of who I was, and then things started to become clear. I could finally get rid of the self-criticism for not measuring up. Now I realize I was just using the wrong measuring stick!

"Now I can find my natural gifts and talents, and appreciate them, and finally accept and love myself! And I love Dressing My Truth! While it makes it easier to shop and know what to buy and what things look good together, the greatest benefit is that it has helped so much in how I feel."

SUMMARY OF THE TYPE 1
BRIGHT, ANIMATED WOMAN

Nitrogen/air is Type 1 energy. A Type 1 woman has an upward, light energy. You are inspiring, fun-loving, and hopeful. Your dominant shape in physical features is the circle and points of a star and is most visible in the eyes, the cheeks, and the overall facial shape.

As a Type 1 woman, you have a tendency towards these strengths:

- You light up the room when you enter it, and are often the life of the party.

- You have an optimistic attitude, and you can see the silver lining even on a cloudy day.

- You have the ability to multitask extremely well, and you can jump from one idea to another in the blink of an eye. Others may find it difficult to keep up with you.

- You have many ideas and can think outside the box. When brainstorming, you may come up with the most ideas and the most creative ways to achieve them.

- You are light-hearted and have an innocence about you that attracts others.

- You look for fun ways to accomplish the things you want to do. Somehow, you can make any job seem fun.

- You are gifted with a brilliant mind that can organize many ideas, events and schedules and move forward with them quickly and efficiently.

- Your energy is light, scattered and upward. It is random in movement and appears to be unstructured and inconsistent to others. This allows you the ability to be flexible, change directions, and be open to new possibilities.

As a Type 1 woman you may have a tendency towards these weaknesses:

- You may have so many ideas that you become overwhelmed with all the possibilities.

- You may choose not to do important but undesirable tasks because they are not fun to you.

- You may move, talk or act before thinking.

- You may appear too scattered or random to accomplish tasks in an orderly manner.

- You may be too light about situations and appear insincere or void of serious thought.

- Your ability to organize things in your mind so quickly and follow through may not appear to be organized to someone who moves forward in a linear pattern.

TYPE 1 BEAUTY KEY WORDS

Active	Innocent
Airy	Inventive
Amusing	Joyous
Animated	Jubilant
Asymmetrical	Light
Beaming	Lively
Bright	Lyrical
Brilliant	Newness
Buoyant	Perky
Candid	Pert
Carefree	Pixie
Casual	Playful
Charming	Precocious
Cheerful	Radiant
Crisp	Rapturous
Effervescent	Refreshing
Enchanting	Renewing
Energetic	Sassy
Exciting	Shining
Expressive	Simple
Exuberant	Spirited
Festive	Sprightly
Flirtatious	Stylish
Fresh	Twinkling
Friendly	Uncomplicated
Frolicsome	Vibrant
Fun-loving	Vital
High Spirited	Vivacious
Idyllic	Vivid
Imaginative	Warm
Informal	Youthful
Ingenious	Zestful

Type 2: The Subtle, Soft Woman

Primary Movement: *Fluid, Flowing*
Natural Gift: *Details—"What do we need to know and do to make the idea possible?"*
Dominant Quality: *Calmly connecting us to our hearts and each other.*
Beauty Code Word: *Beautiful!*

THE TYPE 2 EXPRESSION COMES FROM THE ELEMENT OXYGEN/ WATER, and its natural primary movement is fluid and flowing. If you have a dominant Type 2 movement, you have a fluid, flowing energy. You are naturally calming, inviting, subdued and sensitive. Your dominant shapes in physical features are elongated S curves, ovals and softened rectangles, which is visible in the eyes, the nose, the cheeks, the hairline, and overall body and facial shape.

Type 2 energy is an introvert expression, moving in a subtle and connected flow to create in this world. As a Type 2, you express a medium-to-medium-low movement. This naturally subdued, connected, flowing movement can be consistently observed through aspects of your feminine experience.

Other keywords that describe the movement of this energy in a dominant Type 2 woman are: blended, soft, steady, easy-going, relaxed, connected, nurturing, comforting, warm and detail-oriented.

77

Due to your medium-to-medium low movement that expresses itself calmly, you may have been told a lot as a child and even in your adult life to "Hurry up!" or "Make up your mind!"

Your energy is like the afterglow of a beautiful sunset or the light along the horizon at dawn, creating an ambience of grace, softness and comfort. Your presence adds refinement and grace to the earth. Being in your presence helps us slow down and experience calmness in life. You truly are steady and easy-going, just like the Mississippi River which is just like your element—oxygen/water!

Making sure life is comfortable for yourself and others is a primary motive for a Type 2 woman. Comfort is a priority in every aspect of your life. Acting appropriately so as not to cause any discomfort for others, wearing comfortable clothing, sitting on comfortable furnishings, enjoying comfortable relationships, consuming comforting food, sharing comfortable communication—you name it, comfort is a priority. In all my *Dressing Your Truth*® trainings, I have yet to meet a dominant Type 2 woman that did not have comfort as her number one priority when it came to choosing an article of clothing.

One day, my daughter Anne (Type 2) returned home from shopping having bought herself a new, beautiful sweater. She enthusiastically took her new sweater out of the bag and called me over to feel how comfy it was. Being a dominant Type 3, I did not relate to the value of comfort that she was experiencing and realized that this difference was being created by our very different natural expressions.

ROSSANNE'S STORY

RossAnne reports that when she was first introduced to Dressing Your Truth®, she had no idea who she was, or what Type she was, and felt completely confused and lost. She decided that she should just pick one and talked herself into being a Type 3. Her aunt was in the process of becoming a Dressing Your Truth® Expert, and so she indulged RossAnne's confusion and put Type 3 clothes on her. She thought she looked terrible!

Because her aunt was still learning, she concluded that RossAnne must be a Type 4. RossAnne trusted her and jumped in with both feet, changing her hair, make-up and wardrobe. Then she went through the Dressing Your Truth® training, and was shocked to learn from me and my staff, as they gently guided her to the truth, that she actually led with Type 2.

RossAnne explains: "At first, it was very difficult for me to accept being a dominant Type 2 because it seemed so powerless. I was happy, however, to learn that I did not have to force myself to be friendly and talkative to everyone I met. It was an incredible, amazing experience to embrace my true nature as a Type 2. In fact, it is hard to put into words the way it changed my life!"

RossAnne came to an understanding that has changed literally everything in her life. She continues to be amazed at the transformation she enjoyed, and her life continues to change into something more and more surprising all the time.

"Carol's Dressing Your Truth® was the catalyst I was searching for," RossAnne concludes, "without even realizing I was searching— to discover my true inner self and let that shine! I love myself, I love my life and I am thrilled to know and live my true nature!"

NATURAL GIFTS AND TALENTS

Once the idea has been created—which is initiated by the natural gift of a Type 1 woman—the natural gift of a Type 2 becomes the next phase of the cycle of wholeness by starting the process of asking questions to gather the details. Your energy creates connection and flow. If you were to put your natural gift into a phrase, your phrase would be, **"What do we need to know and do to make the**

idea possible?" It is necessary for you to ask questions and lead out with a degree of skepticism. This supports your need to question whether the possibility could become a reality.

Once the details have been gathered, a Type 2 is able to move forward, figuring out the steps to create a plan that will flow. This process is a tremendous gift to help you to gather, organize and flow with the details. In fact, this is necessary to make an idea a reality!

Important: This is so prominent in your natural expression that it is necessary for you to give yourself time to ask the questions and gather details. Once you have gathered the details, you need to study those details and allow yourself time to process all the contingencies that you feel are valid in order for you to feel comfortable in making a decision and moving forward in your life.

Your sensitivity to details is a remarkable gift. You notice the details that make life flow more smoothly and comfortably for everyone else—like making things look nice, spending a little extra time on wrapping a gift, or presenting a meal you cooked. For example, my Type 2 mother would never let us put the milk carton on the dinner table. Instead, she insisted that the milk be poured into a pitcher and then put on the table so it would be more attractive!

THE GIFT OF THE TYPE 2 WOMAN IS TO CONNECT PEOPLE AT THE HEART.

When you share an experience or tell a story, you include a lot of details. The gift of the Type 2 woman is to connect people at the heart. You offer a sense of peace and calmness to the world.

Growing up with a Type 2 mother was a great gift in my life. To be honest with you, I did not realize the gift my mother gave me and our entire family until I understood the nature of a Type 2 woman. Prior to this understanding, I viewed my mother as somewhat of a doormat. I could not relate to how she managed her life. When I came to understand the nature of a Type 2 woman, I was truly humbled and even brought to tears of gratitude for the gift of my mother's 2-ness.

Having a predominant Type 3 and 4 energy presence in our family due to the Energy Profiles of my dad, brothers and me, it was often a very intense, competitive, and harsh environment in our home. It definitely lacked a playful, light mood since there was no one in my family with a dominant Type 1 energy. What I came to realize, once I understood the gift and power of a Type 2, is that my mother was and is the reason we came through as a family. My mother's gift was to keep us all connected when there were many situations through the years that could have caused us to disconnect.

You move through life like a deep, steady river. You are deliberate and methodical in your approach to life. My youngest daughter Anne is a dominant Type 2. Since Anne was a little girl, she always been attentive to details. At the young age of 2, when she had a messy diaper she would bring me the wipes and a fresh diaper when she needed a diaper change, all without me asking her to do this.

As her Type 3 mother, I truly wish I had known Anne's Type when she was young. I would have stopped moving with such intense determination every day of my life and would have taken more time to just sit and be with her, quietly and comfortably. But as I teach in my book *Remembering Wholeness*, it is never too late to be a good parent. So now, when I am with Anne, I choose to be sensitive to her subtle nature and not over-talk her or push her along too swiftly to make decisions in her life.

Your primary shape is an elongated S curve. The shape of a long winding river, moving deeply, steadily on its course. You can see the relaxed flow of the river in your movement from point A to point B. One of the dominant shapes in your facial features is the elongated S curve, as well as the quality of being blended and subdued in your physical coloring.

You are naturally sensitive. Your softened, subdued movement enables alertness and creates this quality of sensitivity. You are sensitive to how people feel around you. You are sensitive if people feel uncomfortable, and you have a natural gift of inviting them to feel more comfortable. You are sensitive to details and plans. You can even experience sensitivity to foods, chemicals, electronics and subtly toxic environments.

At a recent *Dressing Your Truth*® event, I was assisting a woman who was a dominant Type 2, taking her through a skin analysis. One of the questions is, "Have you experienced any sensitivity to any of the products you have used in the past?" She shared with me her frustration at having what she judged to be overly sensitive skin. I explained to her that her skin's sensitivity was connected to the gift of her 2-ness—the gift of being sensitive and calm, of being aware of people and details, of helping us all feel connected and comfortable. I was not prepared for what happened next, since I thought we were just doing a simple skin profile. Suddenly, she burst into tears and buried her head in her hands. Through her joyful sobs, she shared with me that she finally got it! That what she had been deeming her weakness was actually her greatest gift. I sat there amazed that such a simple interaction could call forth an innate understanding and validation for this woman. Wow. With this, I was beginning to catch on that the *Beauty Profile*℠ system was beautiful and powerful!

The same natural tendencies that are gifts and talents for you can also present a challenge in your life, causing imbalance and disharmony. When your dominant movement is taking over and is not balanced by the other three Types, which are also part of your being, you can be challenged by being you!

Challenge: You can get stuck in the investigation stage where, in asking questions and gathering details, you feel like you need to ask even more questions and gather more details before you can make a decision and move forward.

Challenge: Your tendency to constantly ask questions and seek details can cause you to question yourself and not trust yourself

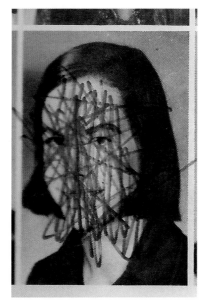

Above left In kindergarten, I was very self-accepting by nature and dressing up was fun!

Above right In seventh grade, my heavy eyebrows looked boyish to me, and I felt very ugly.

Left I recently discovered this picture in my seventh grade yearbook. It brought me to tears when I realized how much I hated the way I looked then, and that I would do this to my picture.

Above I weighed 150 pounds in this high school snapshot, but I might as well have weighed 300 pounds because of the way I felt about myself!

Left Believing I was too fat, I developed an eating disorder during high school and gained 30 pounds.

Left Here I am at 21 and in college, but I was still struggling with my appearance. I feel hotter today even though I am in my 50s!

Lower left This Christmas photo was taken early in my marriage to Jon. I wore a very conservative look then.

Lower right Staying in style in this pose with my 80s perm and a much trimmer body, thanks to working out—a lot!

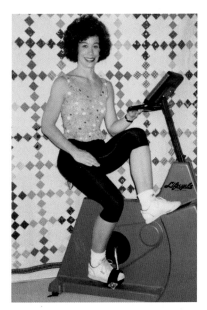

Above Jon and I are with four of our five children—from the left, Mark, Jenny, Anne and Chris. In those days, I was dressing in style but not yet dressing my truth.

Lower left Earlier in life, I was drawn to a lot black, like many women. This dress was stylish for the times, but the contrast of black and white drew attention away from me, the woman in the clothes.

Lower right Here I am dressing my truth today.

Type 1

Bright, Animated Woman

Before   **After**

Type 2

Subtle, Soft Woman

Before   **After**

Type 3

Rich, Dynamic Woman

Before   **After**

Type 4

Bold, Striking Woman

Before   **After**

and your decisions. Due to your more subtle nature, you are not as readily adaptable to change, which can turn into a fear of change.

Challenge: You tend to fuss over details. If this attribute is not channeled in a positive way, you will frequently fuss and worry about life's details, such as money, health and relationships. Find a hobby that allows you to use this natural gift of paying attention to details so you can channel this energy into something that adds value to your life rather than prodding you to worry. My daughter Anne (Type 2) notices her tendency for fussing over the details comes from not channeling her gift for details into something that she enjoys, like cooking and gardening.

PERSONALITY TRAITS

You have a great ability to help people feel connected due to your soft, gentle, relaxed, easy-going way. You encourage other people to relax and take it easy. You connect with people from your heart, which causes you to be very sensitive to how others feel. If someone is feeling down, you are sensitive to that without them even having to share it with you, and then you quietly help them feel better. You will reassure them that everything will be okay in a loving manner.

You move forward in your life with soft and quiet determination. If you are challenged or dealt with too intensely, your tendency is to hold back or go within, feeling the need to retreat in some manner. You will then think about what you may have done to cause this response in another person, often assuming it was your fault.

Again, the dominant element that expresses itself through you is oxygen/water. Phrases commonly used to describe your personality: "You are so easy-going, you just go with the flow," or when it becomes a judgment, "You are so wishy-washy that you can never make up your mind." Your gift of going with the flow can turn into wishy-washiness, like the water that represents your energy!

Challenge: Your priority is not honor and recognition, your priority is to be appropriate to others so they feel comfortable with you. With this tendency, you do not give yourself enough credit when credit is due. Let yourself be in the limelight more often. You deserve it.

Challenge: Your softened, blended, muted energy can cause you to feel like you blend into the background, causing you to feel unimportant. You can feel overlooked and unnoticed.

Challenge: Your personality is naturally sensitive. It would benefit you to pay close attention to your tendency to feel resentment, and your excessive sensitivity in the face of even small humiliations.

Challenge: You can judge your subtle relaxed nature to be weak and wimpy, but the Type 2 movement is a subtle power. The next time you have that thought, just think of the Mississippi River or a mighty willow tree with deep roots and cascading branches and compare yourself to that movement. There is no weakness there, just a deep steady flow, knowing exactly where it is going, winding and bending as it flows along its way. Or the willow standing elegantly in the breeze, offering comfort and support to anyone who sits under its shade to rest and relax for a while.

THOUGHT AND FEELING PROCESSES

Your thoughts follow a steady stream that all connect and make sense. You want a lot of details so you can make these connections in your mind. You need questions answered and details gathered to make a decision. You like to put all the details together to see what the outcome could be. Change can be slower for you, but gathering information and details and thinking it out thoroughly makes change a viable option. You like to think ahead and know what direction things are going.

You like your plans to follow a steady flow. You are not readily adaptable to change. You need time to ask questions and gather details and think things through before you commit to change. You cannot disconnect from your plan and connect with a new plan as readily as the other Types.

Your thoughts are slower and more methodical. You have a continuous process of interconnected thought. You tend to connect the past to the now which then connects to the future. Being told to just live in the Now with no thought to the past or future would be a difficult challenge for you.

My daughter Anne (Type 2) shares that she now understands the nature of her thoughts and just goes with the flow of them. When she was dating with the intent to meet someone and get married, she would go into great detail in her mind about where the relationship might go with every guy she went out with. One thought would lead to the next, which would lead to the next and the next, all the way to wondering if they would marry, how many children they might have, where they might live—and this was all being thought out in her mind before they ever went on the date!

You have many fond memories and love reflecting on your memories. To maintain your connection to the past and your memories of it, you are inclined to create a connection to those memories through keepsakes, photos, scrapbooks and journals. Anne has faithfully kept a daily journal of the details of her life since she was in grade school.

Challenge: You are a more methodical thinker than others who may judge you as slow. You feel it is necessary, first of all, to consider and reconsider everything surrounding a matter until you can form a calm and safe judgment about it.

Challenge: Your attention to detail can turn into brooding, fussing and worrying excessively. Of the four Types, you are the worriers! Remember: worry is a prayer for what you don't want, or an interest payment on a debt that never comes due. Don't get wound around this axle.

Challenge: You can process information over and over in order not to leave anything out, which creates a tendency to get overwhelmed and then find it hard to make a decision.

My daughter Anne (Type 2) and I were on our way to meet my other daughter, Jenny (Type 1), for dinner. My cell phone rang just as we were arriving at our destination and Anne commented, "I bet that is Jenny and she hasn't left yet!"

Yes, it was Jenny and she hadn't left yet! Type 1s have a tendency to be late due to their tendency to get distracted easily. She was calling to offer us another possibility of where to go to dinner. She cheerfully made her suggestion, I told Anne about Jenny's new idea, and Anne replied, "No, I am not going anywhere else. I have already decided what I am going to eat, where we are going to sit, what we might talk about, I have it all planned out in my mind." I told Jenny, "No go. Anne has her mind set on this place."

Since Jenny's energy easily adapts and she is not deeply attached to her ideas, she was fine. As the mother of these two daughters, I was able to honor them both in that moment. I knew it would not offend Jenny to stay with our first idea and that she was just doing her job in offering another possibility. I honored Anne in her Type 2-ness for not being as easily adaptable and having a mindset that thinks things through with many details to consider. We ended up having a lovely evening enjoying each other's company, which includes our similarities and our differences.

COMMUNICATION

You are slower in responding. If you are called upon to answer quickly or to speak without preparation, or if you fear that too much depends on your response, you become restless and do not find the right words and consequently often make a false and unsatisfactory reply.

You have a tendency to assume things and can act like you are correct in your assumption and proceed to respond to the people you are communicating with based on only your assumption. Rather than assume and move forward, share what you are assuming and communicate your assumptions to see how accurate they are.

BEHAVIORAL TENDENCIES

Your behavioral tendencies are expressed like a calm, steady river, moving along methodically in a relaxed, subtle manner following the plans you have made.

RELATIONSHIPS—You value emotional availability, consistency, fiscal responsibility, and accountability in your relationships. You have innate sensitivity to be appropriate so others feel comfortable around you. If I get loud or outspoken in a public setting, it would be common for my daughter Anne or my mom, both Type 2's, to shush me and tell me I am talking too loud. This used to cause me to want to react and get louder, but I now understand their tendency to not want to cause anyone discomfort.

SOCIAL—You are diplomatic, empathetic, proper, meticulous, preferring to observe rather than participate in larger social settings. You have an introverted energy. This does not mean you are shy. That is a label with a negative connotation. An introverted energy means that your energy expresses itself as an inward flow rather than an outward flow. Due to your soft-spoken nature, others may perceive you as shy. I have met a lot of Type 2 women who have been bothered by this judgment of being called shy. They did not feel it was an accurate assessment of who they are. These same women have told me how much they appreciate understanding their more introverted soft nature that has nothing to do with their level of confidence and self-esteem.

In a social setting you will be aware of the sense of community and connection that is occurring or not occurring. You are sensitive to how everyone connects and fits together as a group.

TIMELINESS—You tend to be on time due to your ability to make a plan and stick to it.

WORK—You may appear to others to be slow at your tasks. Yet what you are really doing is working carefully and reliably, but only if you have ample time and are not pressed. You do not see yourself as a slow worker.

You will default to behavior that lets others be preferred over you, even if they are less qualified and capable than you are in a particular kind of work or position, but at the same time you feel slighted because you are being ignored and are assuming your talents are not appreciated.

MONEY—You are great with numbers and taking care of the details of managing money. Due to your meticulous nature and attention to detail, you are good with managing your money, but you can get bogged down by brooding, fretting and worrying about money concerns and having to know where every little cent is going.

PHYSICAL ACTIVITY—You typically plan out your exercise and fitness. You like to have a plan and follow it. You enjoy interacting with others on a more intimate level in your recreational and physical pursuits.

BODY LANGUAGE

Not all of your body language and physical features will express themselves in a Type 2 movement. Most women are blended in their physical features, so you won't see yourself in all these expressions, but you will notice many expressions of body language and physical features that are Type 2 if you are a dominant Type 2 woman.

WALKING— You have a smooth, graceful walk. You take longer steps and keep your feet close to the ground. There is no bounce in your step, rather you have a very fluid, flowing movement.

SITTING/STANDING—You sit and stand in the shape of an S curve. A relaxed bend, holding your head to the side.

VOICE/LANGUAGE—You have a softer voice of medium pitch. You can be hard to hear at times. You may have been told you mumble! You use comforting, nurturing language. You speak in detail and ask many questions.

DOODLING—You doodle in long S curves, ovals and soft relaxed shapes, connecting the shapes together.

PERSONAL SPACE—You are the pile makers. All your piles have a connection and you have an ongoing plan to get rid of the piles. And, when you do, it does not take you long to create new piles! When cleaning you like to take more time to go through things in detail.

You like to keep things that connect you to the memories of the past. My daughter Anne (Type 2) has kept personal items all through her life from her baby blanket, to a favorite sweater from grade school, to making scrapbooks and taking a lot of pictures through the years, all to keep the connections of her memories going.

INTERIOR DESIGN—Comfort is your number one priority in how you decorate your home. You like comfort in all things. Giving attention to detail in your décor and creating a soft, comfortable, cozy environment feels right for you.

PHYSICAL FEATURES

The overall quality of your physical expression is softened and blended. Your bone structure creates elongated S curves and ovals. For visual examples and pictures of Type 2 facial features, please watch the *Beauty Profile*SM course at *www.dressingyourtruth.com*.

SKIN AND SKIN TEXTURE—Type 2 skin is soft and supple with blended skin tones. It is free of wrinkles and lines and as a result you look younger as you age. Type 2 skin drapes beautifully and softly over the bone structure. It is also typical that a dominant Type 2 woman has a very low and subtle contrast in their skin and hair coloring. Women with Type 2 skin maintain a soft, supple appearance to their skin, having the least wrinkles even as they age. My mother who has Type 2 skin does not look her age at all due to her soft, supple skin.

FACE SHAPE—Oval.

CHEEKS—Long S curve, elongated cheek, or dropping cheek, hush puppy cheek.

NOSE—Soft on top, medium size, S curve on side, S curve in the nostrils.

EYEBROWS—Half of an oval, long S curve, very long eyebrows, not very high arch.

EYES—Big almond shaped eyes, doe eyes, dreamy eyes, heavy-lidded or drooping eye lids.

HANDS—Soft, graceful, smooth, long fingers that taper toward nail, oval nail beds.

HOW YOUR ENERGY AFFECTS OTHER PEOPLE

Your energy creates an ambience of calmness and connections. Your fluid, flowing energy relaxes people around you. You are naturally a calming influence to the rest of us. Others experience you as modest and humble. At times, your lower-level of movement can feel slow and draining to others if you are not moving forward in your life, like a log jam in a river that is collecting debris and getting murky.

Your skeptical nature and need to ask questions can cause others to see you as a "doubting Thomas" or a "worry-wart."

As you are conscious of your natural movement and are more aware of who you are interacting with, you will be able to manage yourself in a way that supports others in being in rapport with you. As you stay conscious of who you are and love who you are rather than judge your natural movement and try to silence it, you will be consistently aligned with your core true nature and others will always enjoy being around you.

Now I'll explore some specifics around fashion and a Type 2 woman.

SENDING THE RIGHT MESSAGE: HOW YOUR APPEARANCE AFFECTS OTHER PEOPLE

When you are not dressing your truth, you send a message that conflicts with who you truly are. Your nature is to be gentle and calm and when you wear clothes that make you appear more aggressive, your true nature is disguised to most people, and you can often be judged as wimpy and weak. Type 2 women often think, "If I dress more soft and subtle, I will come across as weak!" This is not the case. When you dress your truth, your inner truth is in harmony with your outer appearance and you will be taken seriously for who you are: a subtle, soft, powerful woman.

Even in a professional setting where you want to be seen as a woman of confidence and strength, putting on a more aggressive look is not in your best interest. When you learn to dress your truth, you learn that you can still look incredibly professional and maintain your softness.

What you are wearing sends a message to other people which influences their first impression of you. You may be judged in a negative light because your true nature is not being honored by your appearance. You have a gift of bringing calmness and connection to any situation. Set the mood everywhere you go by dressing your truth and letting your gentleness express itself in your outer appearance.

MOST COMMON FASHION MISTAKES

It is common for a Type 2 woman to have a tendency to want to brighten her look to counter her more subdued nature. Ironically, it only makes her blend into the background while her brighter clothes get all the attention. Wearing bright and bold clothing will overpower a Type 2 woman, make her complexion look pasty, and actually make her appear weak and shy to people.

I have met a lot of Type 2 women that try and brighten up their hair color with warm highlights that only age their faces, bringing out wrinkles and redness in their skin. Also straightening your hair stick straight is not pretty on you. Your movement has a natural inward flow, and stick straight hair is too severe.

One of our *Dressing Your Truth*® clients came to a training with shoulder length hair that she had parted down the middle and wore straight. I showed her how to part her hair on the side, flipping her hair to fall from the top of her head in a soft S curve around her face, and we used the flat iron to create a soft curl flowing inward toward her face at the ends of her hair. The difference was remarkable—it was like an instant face-lift!

SHOPPING TENDENCIES

Because you have to think things through and you question yourself, it can be challenging to make fashion choices you are confident with. Two of your most common tendencies when it comes to shopping are (1) questioning yourself after you make a purchase and asking others if it is right for you; and (2) leaving the price tags on the clothes, even if you wear it a time or two, just in case it is not right and you decide to return it.

My daughter Anne (Type 2) recently discovered that she and my mom (Type 2) both have this price tag tendency. I have discovered this is common for a lot of Type 2 women. My mom dresses her truth as a Type 2 and looks amazing. She is in her late 70s and appears a good 15 years younger than she is. I have gotten used to her tendency whenever I visit her to want me to see her newest fashion purchases and then to ask me if they are right for her. They always are, and I believe she knows it, but due to her questioning nature she can't help it! I always tell her she is right on with her choices and that she looks remarkable!

Probably your most telling aspect of your shopping experience is your strong sense of whether or not shoes or articles of clothing feel comfortable to you. You first touch a garment to determine if it is even comfortable enough to try on. Once it has passed your comfort touch test, you put it on and move around in it, touch it some more and then decide if it meets your high standard of comfort. If the garments or shoes do not meet your standard, back on the shelf they go. If you try and convince yourself it's comfortable enough and you buy it, most likely it will be returned to the store shortly! Whenever I compliment my mom and how great she looks, she will always respond with a comment about her clothes or shoes with a statement like this, "And it is so comfortable!"

THE TYPE 2 WOMAN BEAUTY CODE WORD

Every woman is remarkably beautiful, no matter what Type she is. Your natural feminine expression lends itself for you to have a certain kind of beauty that depicts the Type of woman you are. When *Dressing Your Truth*® and honoring your truest beauty, a Type 2 woman will be told a lot "You are so beautiful!" Yes, the beauty code word for a Type 2 woman is *Beautiful!*

Your natural expression of gentleness and elegance fits the most commonly used word to compliment an attractive woman—*beautiful*. You have a romantic, graceful quality that expresses itself to the world when you are *Dressing Your Truth*®, so you will hear this a lot, "You are such a beautiful woman."

YOUR BEAUTY SIXTH SENSE DRESSING YOUR TRUTH TIP

You have a natural instinct for comfort, and it is your nature to be very aware if something is comfortable to you. Your sensitivity to comfort needs to be honored in how you dress and accessorize. If what you are putting on your body is not comfortable to you, it is going against your beauty sixth sense. I am sure you already do this, but now you can do it with greater honor and respect for your more sensitive nature. Be sure to ask yourself these questions when you are trying something on, "Does it feel comfortable?" and "Does it support my sensitive nature?" If you can say yes, you are honoring your beauty sixth sense.

FAMOUS TYPE 2 WOMEN

Jessica Alba, Jennifer Aniston, Toni Braxton, Hillary Clinton, Hilary Duff, Jennifer Hudson, Grace Kelly, Angela Lansbury, Shelley Long,

Princess Diana of Wales, Julia Roberts, Jane Seymour, Jaclyn Smith, Barbra Streisand, and Emma Thompson.

―――――――――

ANNETTE'S STORY

I'm going to let Annette tell her story in her own words.

"*I first became acquainted with Dressing Your Truth® in March 2008. I signed up for the class with absolutely no idea of what I was getting into, other than the fact it was offered by Carol Tuttle! My sister had introduced me to Remembering Wholeness by Carol several months previously, so I knew whatever the class was about, it would be compelling!*

"*Imagine my surprise when I arrived at the class, and found I was going to learn more about my beauty Type, and how to support my true self. The idea of supporting my true self was very intriguing to me, because I had been praying for several months to change my thought patterns and heal myself from a pattern of anxiety and fear. I had made significant progress, but was feeling stuck again.*

"*As I began learning about the four different Types of women, I immediately recognized that I had many characteristics of a Type 2. My thought patterns are very connected. I get very caught up in details. When someone proposes a project, my mind immediately jumps to the specifics of how we are going to accomplish that task. Prior to learning about Profiling, I often described myself as a logistical thinker. I could relate to the idea that I am connected and comfortable. However, I was uncomfortable with many aspects of a Type 2. I did not consider myself as elegant, graceful, romantic, or even easy and relaxed. I remember thinking, 'I don't want to be subtle and blended. If I am a Type 2, I might as well not exist, because no one will ever notice me. I will just blend in and disappear.'*

"Over the next two and a half days, I gained more understanding of the Types, and how to support myself. I accepted that I am a Type 2. (Or at least I thought I did!) I learned what colors and design lines support me. I must admit, at first I really didn't like the colors that support a 2. I remember looking at the rack of boring, bland clothing and thinking, "I sure hope those aren't the clothes for a 2. I wouldn't be caught dead in those clothes." Obviously, those were the Type 2 clothes!

"I decided to have a positive attitude, and see if there was truth in this experience that I needed to learn. I immersed myself in the process, and tried the clothing on. I actually found there was clothing I really liked! I loved my transformation. I felt beautiful! But on day three, I melted down. I found myself crying during the middle of our class. Learning all these new things about myself was very unsettling. I knew deep in my heart that I was a Type 2, but I still didn't want to be. I really felt that if I embraced being a 2, I would become lost to the rest of the world. No one would ever notice or see me. I realized I really hadn't accepted myself for who I am.

"I took the challenge given at the end of the class, and chose to exclusively dress like a 2 for 30 days. I have never looked back. I had lost 35 plus pounds several months prior to attending Dressing Your Truth®. Very few people had noticed. Once I began dressing my truth I had many, many people tell me how fabulous I looked and ask me how much weight I had lost recently!

"Knowing my Type of beauty has been a life-changing experience for me. I have learned who I really am, and I love it! I love me! Having this knowledge about myself has validated me. Changing my outward appearance is only a tiny part of the changes I have experienced. In fact, it is probably the least important aspect of my transformation. I feel whole and complete now that I know myself. The Beauty Profiling^{SM} and Dressing Your Truth® systems have been an integral part of my journey over the last year to change my thought patterns and become the woman God created me to be."

MILANA'S STORY

After Milana (Type 2) went through the Dressing Your Truth® train-ing, all the information seemed to strongly indicate that she was a Type 1. "Of course!" she says. "Energetic, spontaneous, playful— that's me."

She joined the chatty group of Type 1s after the class and real-ized that she was the only one who was silent. She loved being in that group, but was only a listener and observer.

I came up to Milana and assessed her physical features and told her that she might be in the wrong group and to consider that she might be a Type 2!

She was shocked. She didn't enjoy the company of those gloomy, self-absorbed Type 2s. Or so she thought.

When she began rereading the tendencies for a Type 2, she began thinking and questioning herself. She looked at the clothes desig-nated for Type 2s, and decided she loved all of them. But as for the clothes for a Type 1, she did not like a single piece.

She began to realize that she loved the company of Type 1s so much that she just wanted to be one of them. She wanted to be energetic, spontaneous and playful. But in real life, she wasn't that way. It was quite a discovery for her. Slowly, she started to see the positive traits of Type 2s. She stopped trying to be someone else and started to be more of who she really was.

MICHELLE'S STORY

Michelle bought the online Dressing Your Truth® course for Type 2s and watched it, and as soon as she heard the keywords soft and gentle, she started crying. It brought up a lot of issues for her.

Growing up, her father wanted boys and never got any, so he called his five daughters his "boys." She also saw her mother and grandmothers dominated by Type 3 and 4 men. When she was younger, she decided that she wouldn't live that way and have anyone dominate her, so she admits that she became more bold and forceful—all of the negative traits of a Type 3 and 4.

But since she has been dressing her truth, she says she has never felt better about herself! She now says that she feels so soft and feminine, and it's a good thing! She says she has been nicer to her husband and children, and for the first time in 15 years, she actually likes the way she looks and is not embarrassed to go out and be seen, even though she is overweight.

She was surprised that dressing her truth and finding out what Type of woman she is has been so freeing.

"I've used a lot of self-help tools for years that have helped me with a lot of my issues," she says, "but it's interesting to me how this process has helped me to become happier and more myself than anything else I've ever tried before. It's even brought up issues that I didn't realize I even had."

SUMMARY OF THE TYPE 2
SUBTLE, SOFT WOMAN

Oxygen/water is Type 2 energy. A Type 2 woman has a fluid and flowing energy. You are detail-oriented, easy-going, and are a sensitive, go-with-the-flow Type. Your dominant shape in physical features is a soft flowing S curve, an oval and a softness that is visible in your eyes, cheeks and overall facial shape.

As a Type 2 woman you may have a tendency toward these strengths:

- You have a gift of steadiness. Your strength is the steadiness and consistency you offer to others.

- You are gentle and create a soft, comfortable, safe environment.

- You are methodical in your work and absorb all the details that others may not see.

- You are kind-hearted and patient, allowing for life to flow at its pace.

- You are a connector. Connecting people, ideas, places, businesses and happenings.

- You are subtle and your strength is in the quiet determination you bring to everything.

- You are detailed, conscientious and methodical.

- You are a peacemaker: gentle, soft, kind and sweet.

- You can see another's point of view and understand where they are coming from.

- You can accomplish many things in a calm, quiet, subtle way that is unobtrusive.

As a Type 2 woman you may have a tendency towards these weaknesses:

- You may get caught up in all the details and find it difficult to make decisions.

- You may be too attached to people, things, or memories and not be willing to let go so you can move forward in life.

- You may appear to be too soft, too nice and not be able to stand your ground and share your true feelings.

- You may become so concerned about others' feelings that you don't acknowledge your own or give yourself value.

- You may require others to slow down because you think, like you, they need to move in a slower pattern and give more attention to details before moving forward.

TYPE 2 BEAUTY KEY WORDS

Blended	Luxurious
Careful	Meticulous
Classical	Modest
Comfortable	Muted
Composed	Mysterious
Conscientious	Neat
Consistent	Particular
Courtly	Penetrating
Delicate	Picturesque
Demure	Placid
Detailed	Pleasing
Dignified	Poised
Diplomatic	Prudent
Dreamy	Quaint
Elegant	Queenly
Ethereal	Refined
Exacting	Relaxed
Exquisite	Retiring
Fastidious	Romantic
Fine	Semi-formal
Finesse	Sensitive
Finished look	Serene
Flowing	Silky
Fluid	Simple
Gentleness	Soft
Graceful	Soothing
Harmonized	Suave
Heavenly	Subtle
Innocent	Sumptuous
Intricate	Sweet
Inviting	Traditional
Lavish	Warmness
Lovely	Well-groomed
Luscious	Wise

TYPE 3: THE RICH, DYNAMIC WOMAN

Primary Movement: *Active, Reactive*
Natural Gift: *Action—"Let's get to work and get it done!"*
Dominant Quality: *Swiftly moving us forward to our desired outcomes.*
Beauty Code Word: *Hot!*

THE TYPE 3 EXPRESSION COMES FROM THE ELEMENT HYDROGEN/ FIRE, and its natural primary movement is active/reactive. If you have a dominant Type 3 movement, you have an active/reactive energy. You are naturally dynamic, sure and purposeful. Your dominant shapes in your physical features are angles, triangles and asymmetrical shapes, which are visible in the eyes, the nose, the cheeks, the hairline, and overall body and facial shape.

Type 3 energy is an extrovert expression pushing forward with intensity to create in this world. As a Type 3 you express a medium to medium-high level of movement. This natural, dynamic, deliberate and purposeful movement can be consistently observed through aspects of your human experience.

Other key words that describe the movement of this energy in a dominant Type 3 woman are swift, substantial, rich, textured, intense, practical, resourceful, to-the-point, fiery and abrupt.

Due to your medium to medium-high movement that expresses itself deliberately, you may have been told a lot as a child, and even in your adult life, to "Relax!" or "You're too demanding," or "Pipe down! You're too loud."

Your energy is like the dynamic push of Niagara Falls, as I mentioned earlier, or the substantial depth and texture of the Grand Canyon, leaving a lasting impression with the results you create. You truly are a ball of fire, like the great fireball, the sun, made up of the same element as your Dominant Type—hydrogen/fire!

Taking action to get a result is a primary motive for a Type 3 woman. Results are a priority in how you approach life. Action that creates results and change are important to you. Because your energy is active/reactive in its nature, your motive in your actions is to create a result that makes an impression that remains for a long time, just like the action of the Colorado River carving a lasting impression we call the Grand Canyon! Ironically, you are not innately motivated to do what you do to impress other people—that is just an outcome that naturally happens due to your dynamic energy.

When I was 15 years old, I had an experience that would have helped me better understand myself, if there had been a *Beauty Profile*SM system to refer to at the time. I had long hair below my shoulders then, and one day I abruptly decided I wanted to get it cut. I had been given a coupon for a free haircut at the local beauty school. Since I couldn't drive and my mom and dad were out of town, I left school early, walked home (which was about three miles away), jumped on my bike and rode it 10 miles across town to the beauty school. I didn't have an appointment but, fortunately, they did take walk-ins. I got my haircut in a completely new style, cutting a lot of my hair off. I rode my bike home and just "got it done"! I think of that now and that screams Type 3 all over the place. Just get it done! There are so many great clues all through our lives that point to who we truly are.

When you have your mind set on your results, your inner mantra is "to do whatever it takes" and you are willing to roll up your sleeves, get to work, and just get things done.

When I started my business 20 years ago, I wore all the hats. I had to rely on the expression of all four Types to launch my business—the ideas, the details, the action, and the refining process. What kept me motivated was the result I had my sights set on. Even though I played all the parts, I definitely led with my Type 3 energy through the experience.

I was willing to burn the candle at both ends since my actions were being driven by a strong desire to create results. At the same time I started building my business, I had young children and I would not compromise my standards on being a good mother. This looked like a lot of late nights and early mornings to do whatever it required to achieve the results I was determined to create. I did not think much of it. In my mind, it was just what I had to do.

It would bother me to be labeled a driven person or to be seen as too big of a thinker. I did not understand why I did not relate to most of the women in my neighborhood, who seemed so satisfied with being full-time moms. I have always had some entrepreneurial venture going on and now I understand that it was my natural ability to think big and go for it!

I have also come to realize that Type 3s have the capacity to "burn ourselves out" more quickly than any other Types due to our swift, determined movement, which is being fueled by our pronounced, substantial energy output. I have gotten into more things with great passion, going big fast and then grew bored and moved on to my next big life experience.

For example, I started running marathons in 2001. I went on to run 16 marathons over the next four years. One day in November 2005, I just decided I was done, like Forrest in the movie Forrest Gump: he ran and ran and ran, and then just out of nowhere, he stopped and felt complete with the experience. That is a very Type 3 movement! I created a lasting impression, though, with all my marathon T-shirts and medals, and it seems to be impressive to people, yet impressing people was never my motive in going for the results I did. I did it because I have come to learn it is my Type 3 nature that likes to experience life big and swift!

Type 3 and Type 4 energy are very dynamic, bold energy expressions. They have not been considered feminine in their nature in our culture of the past. Some women can confuse whether they are a dominant Type 3 or 4 since both expressions are very strong.

DEBBIE'S STORY

Debbie felt in conflict. She identified herself as a Type 4 at a live Profiling training. When the Beauty Profiling[SM] *Experts explained to her that she was actually a Type 3 with a strong secondary 4, she disagreed. (Of course she would; she is a Type 3!) It took her a few days, but the more she thought about it and considered it, the more sense it made.*

She had always thought she should be the Type of person that Type 4s are. Any good person would be a Type 4, she thought. She recognized that there is a lot of Type 4 in her and that sometimes being a 4 is what feels natural, but most of the time, she admits that she tried to force herself to be a 4 when she was actually feeling more like a Type 3.

Debbie says: "The most amazing and miraculous thing this information did for me was to help me realize that whatever I am is good—better than just good—I am wonderful, just naturally as I am. I don't have to force myself to be any particular way. I already am what I am, and can just relax into it. I'm really not expected to be something else."

NATURAL GIFTS AND TALENTS

In the cycle of wholeness we have noted that Type 1 energy initiates the cycle with an idea, the Type 2 energy gathers the details by asking questions and making a plan, and the Type 3 moves us into action. Your Type 3 energy moves into action swiftly to make things happen to create a result. If you were to put your natural gift into a phrase, your phrase would be "Let's get to work and get it done!"

As much as Type 1s love starting new things, Type 3s love finishing things they start. As a Type 3, you actually only start something that you are motivated to finish, so you can experience the result of your actions. And you don't just start one thing: you have the capacity to push several things along at a time and make sure they all get done. My daughter-in-law Sarah (Type 3) and I started to compare notes when she joined the family a few years ago. Since I do not have any of my own Type 3 children, my only reference within my family had been myself. I play pretty big for a Type 3 due to my secondary Type 4.

One thing Sarah and I both noted was how we get multiple tasks moving forward at the same time, so we can get a lot of things done at once. A typical morning would look like this: taking a shower, starting to get dressed, abruptly stopping to make the bed, moving to the kitchen to start loading the dishwasher, back to dressing, abruptly moving again to the bed, kitchen, dressing—keeping a lot of plates spinning until all the tasks are finished. If I were to trace my movement, it would create a lot of intersecting lines making geometric shapes and fast angles, and compartments. Exactly the movement I doodle in, dress in, and express my natural self in!

My son Chris (Type 2) and Sarah (Type 3) were dating around the time I was developing *Dressing Your Truth®*. At the time, I couldn't tell what Sarah's Dominant Type was. She is very blended in her movement and facial features, and it was quite a mystery to me.

We had not introduced the Profiling information to her, and it has always been my rule of thumb not to tell people their Type. I began to notice her tendencies as she spent more time in our home. One incident really stood out and was very telling for me. Chris and Sarah came in early from a date and were talking about what to do next. I heard Sarah say to Chris, "Please, let's just clean out the car so I can check it off my list for the day!" Chris replied "It can wait. Let's just relax and take it easy for a while. We've been going all day long."

True to both their natures, in Sarah's 3-ness she was interested in completing the tasks on her list, to get the results she had her mind set on, and Chris in his 2-ness was encouraging them to relax and to find comfort for the remainder of the evening.

Sarah and I joke that we will write on our to-do lists tasks we have already accomplished just for the satisfaction of checking them off the list!

We also noticed one Christmas how we both have a tendency to sit back and gaze at our Christmas trees after we finish decorating them. We realized that it is common for Type 3s to gain so much pleasure in creating a result that we will set aside time to take it in and bask in the pleasure of just looking at the result we accomplished!

You move through life like a tiger, with a very stable, deliberate movement. You jump in and take action quickly. You see what needs to get done, and often wonder why no one else is taking action, assuming the rest of the world moves in your expression.

YOU ARE A READY-FIRE-AIM PERSON.

You can push a lot of things forward at once, moving yourself and other people into action. You are the *ready-fire-aim* person, and sometimes that can burn you and others out. Your primary movement is swift, with intersecting, connected lines that create compartments. Rather than moving on one track from point A to point B, you have at least three or more tracks at a time that you move things forward on. This movement would create a textured surface, which likewise is a physical feature in Type 3 skin.

You can change focus abruptly, but you always come back to what you have started. You are very aware of what has gone unfinished, and that you can spur you into action and cause an abrupt change of focus.

Important: It is important that you acknowledge and allow your energy to have a swift, pushing nature. If you try to soften your movement and override it with apologies, it can be like a burning furnace that has no vent and will suddenly go into reactive mode—what we call rage! When you do not allow your Dominant Type to lead in your expressive self, you lose your connection with who you are. You will be out of balance from your active/reactive energy if you try to soften or sedate yourself.

The same natural tendencies that are your gift and talents can also be a challenge in your life, causing imbalance and disharmony. While you lead with your dominant energy, when your dominant movement is taking over your life and is not balanced with the other three Types (which are also a part of your being), it can be a challenge being you!

Challenge: An impediment for a Type 3 can be your yearning for great things with imprudent haste. You can become immediately absorbed by the aim you have in mind and rush for your goal with great acceleration and impetuosity. You consider too little whether you can really reach your goal because you are so sure of yourself.

Challenge: You like to create a reaction from your actions. If you are not consciously allowing your substantial energy to be expressed in a healthy way, you may be subconsciously creating scenarios where you are saying and doing things just to get a reaction out of people, and most of the time it will appear to be contentious!

Growing up, I had no reference to what a Type 3 woman was like. I was being exposed to a lot of Type 3 and 4 men, since my dad and brothers express a lot of this energy. My mom, being a Type 2, was not a reference for me. The church I attended appeared to craft the image of the ideal woman and mom to be either a Type 1 or 2 expression. Not having any conscious knowledge of my inner nature, I was not able to manage it consciously to add quality to my life.

It now makes sense to me why I have been the catalyst for so many arguments with my Type 2 husband. I just wanted to experience my active/reactive nature.

SHEILA'S STORY

Because she felt at one time less than beautiful, Sheila says that the Beauty Profile^SM system has been invaluable to her. She wanted a cute little nose and thought that a nose job would do it, but she could never bring herself to go through with it. She saw all the many flaws in herself, but then she would feel guilty for having those feelings. "I guess I just told myself that my appearance was as good as it was going to get," she says. "And that I should work on being the best me I can be."

When she went through her Dressing Your Truth® transformation, a miracle occurred. Her edgy haircut actually made her nose seem just right for her face. The perceived flaws were gone! She finally understood why she had certain features and how to make them just that—features, not flaws. They are beautiful features, part of her nature, made just for her.

She writes: "I remember writing my testimonial [of Dressing Your Truth®] and just letting my pen flow with no restraint. I wrote that I found myself again, a happy person who finally saw my beauty inside and out. I felt like I was starting to see myself as God sees me. It was too good of a feeling to justly describe."

Sheila has been dressing her truth for one year, and she feels that it has been amazing. She says, "I like the way I look. I like the way I feel. I have lost two dress sizes though I haven't changed my diet! Perfect strangers stop to tell me how great I look. They usually notice one thing, but then they can't pick out just one, so they will wave their hands up and down and go with the whole look. 'Perfect!' I haven't grown tired of it, and I don't plan on it! My family loves it. My teenage daughters' friends tell them that their mom is hot! Could be worse, right?"

PERSONALITY TRAITS

Action that creates results and lasting change or impressions are important to you as a Type 3. You measure results and base your success on whether or not the measured results are congruent with projected results. You can act before all the details are in place, often feeling like so many details are unnecessary as you have a deep sense of confidence and sureness about achieving success. You are very expressive about what results have been or will be achieved in your life. You can change directions abruptly and can handle diverse situations and many goals at once.

You move other people into action easily. If someone is feeling down, you will think of something to do to help the person change focus or what you can do to help fix it. You move forward with intense determination.

The dominant element that is expressing in you is hydrogen/fire. Phrases commonly used to describe your personality are, "You are dynamic," or when it becomes a judgment, "You are too pushy and intense."

The two personal trainers on the hit show The Biggest Loser are both dominant Type 3 energies. Both Jillian Michaels and Bob Harper are passionate about helping people get massive results in losing weight. If you want to see Type 3 energy at its best, watch this show. They have a fiery push in getting people to work harder than they have ever worked in their life to reach their dreams. They are not acting! It is their active/reactive energy coming through. To help someone lose over 150 pounds in a few months takes a Type 3!

Challenge: You can burn out by getting too much going on, making too many commitments, and taking action too soon.

Type 3 women are very passionate. Whenever you are bent about carrying out your plans, or find opposition, you are filled with passionate excitement. You can become addicted to action! If someone challenges you or suggests you can't do what you are desiring to do, you most likely are thinking, "Oh yeah, just watch me!" You are very self-confident and self-reliant and tend to take success for granted because you expect it.

You have the most competitive nature of all the Types, with the Type 4 energy close behind you. You are just as competitive with yourself as you are with an opponent.

Challenge: You can be impetuous and impulsive in a big way, plunging into situations where more forethought would have benefited you.

THOUGHT AND FEELING PROCESSES

Your thoughts and feelings are swift and deliberate. You compartmentalize your thoughts to keep track of all the activities you have put into motion. You compartmentalize things in your head and can move from one compartment to the next easily, without losing concentration because it all has a purpose to you.

You do not like to take time to read instructions in detail as you have confidence that you will be able to figure it out as you go. You think first about the result and outcome to be achieved rather than what it will take to get there. You like to move into action quickly.

Challenge: Because you have an active/reactive nature, you can be very reactive when you are emotionally triggered. You may abruptly and intensely say what you are feeling and it may come across as harsh. Giving yourself a moment to cool off and process your emotions without reacting so intensely is important to you. You will be heard and understood more fully when you can share how you feel when you are more at ease.

COMMUNICATION

You value honest communication, credibility and realism. You like to get to the point in your communication. In fact, a common phrase you will use when someone is dragging things out is, "What's your point?" Going over too many details can bog you down.

When in authority—which is often the case!—you are good at delegating. When you feel someone is credible and they get results, you give them free rein to do what you have delegated to them. You don't like to beat around the bush, and you are practical and honest in your communications.

You value your accomplishments, the results you create in life. You like talking about your results and accomplishments readily. It may appear to others that you are bragging, but results are such a central focus of your movement that you don't think of it as bragging. Since you are not motivated by impressing people, it surprises you when people think of you this way.

BEHAVIORAL TENDENCIES

Your behavioral tendencies model that of a hawk, circling the prey, moving along deliberately with your eye on the result you want, spotting opportunities, and moving swiftly or diving into action to create it.

RELATIONSHIPS—You are open in your relationships, eager to work things out with your loved ones. You express a great deal of love and affection for the select people you form deeper relationships with.

SOCIAL—You have the confidence to interact with anyone. You are friendly and talkative in social situations. You are a natural sales person.

TIMELINESS—You may have a tendency for being late due to your tendency to want to get so much done. You are not realistic about what can be finished in the time allotted, but you will try to do it anyway. Being late sets the stage for you to move into swift action, getting done what you want before you leave for your destination.

WORK—You are reliable. You excel in positions that allow you to take the lead, motivate others, and challenge your entrepreneurial spirit. It is common for a Type 3 woman to pursue an entrepreneurial opportunity in their professional career. Type 3s are not afraid of the risk of doing their own thing due to their high level of confidence. Your reputation reflects that confidence, and people say of you, "You can count on her to get the job done."

> **Challenge:** You tend to dominate people of other Types in work settings, especially Type 2s.

MONEY—You are good with money and have a strong focus on it. Money is a measurement of your results in your professional activities. The more money you are making, the more you are getting the results you want with your profession or business pursuits.

PHYSICAL ACTIVITY—You prefer group activities and competition. You love to challenge yourself and win. You are a very physical woman, enjoying everything from exercise or adventure trips. Years ago I was getting bored with my daily exercise routine. That is when I started to train for marathons. I found that as a Type 3, I was more motivated to get up early and train for an event that I wanted to be prepared for, rather than to just exercise without a bigger goal.

Since I have given up marathon running, I switched to competing in sprint-distance triathlons. Last year, I had a goal to compete in one triathlon a month from April through November. I successfully met my goal and had a lot of fun doing it. I have noticed that most of the people competing in triathlons are Type 3s, especially in the women's divisions.

BODY LANGUAGE

Not all of your body language and physical features will express in a Type 3 movement. Most women are blended in their physical features, so you won't see yourself in all these expressions, but you will notice many expressions of body language and physical features that are Type 3 if you are a dominant Type 3 woman.

WALKING—You walk with a determination in your step, with a firm plant of your feet, quick and brisk. Everyone can hear you coming.

SITTING/STANDING—Others can hear when you sit, due to your deliberate movement. You create angles when you sit and stand. You will often have your legs crossed, or one leg pulled up under you, your head cocked to the side, hands on waist, or your body bent at the waist.

VOICE/LANGUAGE—A Type 3 voice is brassy with a medium to low pitch. You can speak explosively in volume at times. Your language can be intense, reactive, abrupt and sassy.

DOODLING—You doodle using shapes that represent your natural movement, that is, angles and asymmetrical shapes in all directions.

PERSONAL SPACE—You know where everything is due to how you can compartmentalize things in your mind. You can have a lot out and around on counters or tables, for example, but can get it cleaned up swiftly. You don't mind cleaning up after yourself because the mess enabled you to experience the result of the effort expended. Due to your practical nature, what you own needs to be useful to you. You may be known for getting rid of things too quickly, such as throwing away your children's homework.

INTERIOR DESIGN—You prefer your surroundings to be casual, natural and rich in color and texture.

PHYSICAL FEATURES

The overall quality of your physical expression is earthy, textured, natural and exotic. Your bone structure has angles and is chiseled giving a look of strength with your features being asymmetrical. For visual examples and pictures of Type 3 facial features, please see the Type 3 *Beauty Profile*SM course at *www.dressingyourtruth.com*.

SKIN AND SKIN TEXTURE—Type 3 skin has an irregular pigment, sunspots, age spots, rough, textured, deeper lines, and can be prone to acne. If you have Type 3 skin, you may have been investing time and money trying to eliminate the natural features of your 3-ness expressing in your skin.

I have Type 3 skin, which is a higher, more textured movement, which expresses itself in my skin as hyper-pigmentation, more creases, and texture. I have come to learn that it is best to work with this expression and support bringing out the natural beauty of my skin rather than trying to change it. When I am dressing my truth and have a hairstyle in the right color, cut and style, I enhance the appearance of my skin by having the right movement and vibration around my face. The result is that the features in my skin that

I once saw as a flaw, I now experience as naturally beautiful and I feel gratitude for those features.

FACE SHAPE—Triangular, angular facial planes, square or angular jaw, chiseled edges.

CHEEKS—Various forms of triangles on cheeks and/or around mouth; high, chiseled cheekbones.

NOSE—Angular, beak, knobby, lump of clay, with triangular nostrils.

EYEBROWS—Come to a peak somewhere after the middle of the eye.

EYES—Come to a point in the inside of eye or outside corners, angles above the eyes in the lid area to create a very exotic look.

HANDS—Rough, textured, knobby knuckles, spots, veiny, with lots of pigmentation. It is common for a Type 3 with Type 3 hands to comment that they think their hands look old due to these features.

HOW YOUR ENERGY AFFECTS OTHER PEOPLE

Your energy leaves an impression, which makes you noticed by others. Your active/reactive energy moves people into action. You are naturally a leader to others. You may notice that family and friends turn to you to take the lead to make decisions and lead out.

For example, on a family vacation, you may be the one who decides which activities to do each day and gets everybody moving in that direction. When we were having dinner out one night with a large number of our family members, my daughter-in-law Sarah (Type 3), who was very new to the family, noticed the need to decide what flavor and sizes of pizzas to order. She naturally took charge of getting the group to make the decision and called the waitress over to place the order. At times, others can experience your energy as overbearing, pushy and insensitive. You can be judged as being too much to handle or misperceived as overconfident.

Now I'll explore some specifics around fashion and a Type 3 woman.

SENDING THE RIGHT MESSAGE: HOW YOUR APPEARANCE AFFECTS OTHER PEOPLE

When you are not dressing your truth, you send a message that is in conflict with who you truly are. Your nature is to be dynamic and determined, and when you wear clothes that make you appear to be soft and quiet, your true nature is disguised to most people and it will come across as unexpected and can often be judged as aggressive and pushy. Type 3 women often think, "If I dress more dynamic and edgy, I will come across too intense." This is not the case. When you dress your truth, your inner truth is in harmony with your outer appearance and you will be taken seriously for who you are: a rich, dynamic woman.

Even in a professional setting where you want to be seen as a woman who is passionate and caring, putting on a softer look is not in your best interest. When you learn to dress your truth, you learn that you can still look incredibly professional and stay true to your dynamism.

What you are wearing sends a message to other people, which influences their first impression of you. You may be judged in a negative light because your true nature is not being honored by your appearance. You have a gift of bringing decisiveness and action to any situation. Set the mood everywhere you go by dressing your truth and letting your dynamism express itself clearly in your outer appearance.

MOST COMMON FASHION MISTAKES

It is common for a Type 3 woman to have a tendency to be drawn to and wear a lot of black. Type 3 energy is a strong expression and the color black makes a strong statement. The problem is that Type 3 women have very angular, chiseled, textured movement in their physical features which is quite the opposite of the stark, still nature of black. Wearing black, especially around the face, dramatically ages a Type 3 woman.

Before I started dressing my truth, about 65 percent of my wardrobe was black. I no longer own any black clothes. You might think, "How could I give up my black?" I promise you when you go through the *Dressing Your Truth*® course and discover the rich, dynamic colors that express your true nature, you will not miss the black. You will actually get to a point in wondering why you ever wore it!

Another tendency is to want to soften your facial features by wearing soft lines in your hairstyle around your face. This will only make the angular bone structure in your face more pronounced to give you a manly appearance.

SHOPPING TENDENCIES

Your primary motive when you shop is to get it done swiftly and to get the best deal. You love a good deal. You are practical in your nature, so you are practical with your purchases. You love sharing with others what you paid for something when you found a great deal! If someone compliments a garment you happen to have found at a low price, you'll reply to the compliment by saying "I only paid $10.99 for it, isn't that amazing?"

You have to watch out that your practical nature doesn't turn into being cheap! You can go overboard with saving money and holding back from spending money on what might be an important, lasting piece in your new wardrobe.

I have met many Type 3 women who think, "I can figure out how to dress my truth without having to pay for Carol's course!" You actually like the challenge of trying to figure it out, and true to your nature, think you don't need all the details, and also think it is great you are saving money, but you are left without the details and tools you need to bring out your best, most amazing look.

Be willing to take the time to invest in yourself and the *Dressing Your Truth®* information, it will serve you for your entire life, and when you look at the cost of that, you are getting a super great deal!

THE TYPE 3 WOMAN BEAUTY CODE WORD

Every woman is remarkably beautiful, no matter what Type she is. Your natural feminine expression lends itself for you to have a certain kind of beauty that depicts the Type of woman you are. When you are dressing your truth and honoring your truest self and beauty, you as a Type 3 woman will be told often, "You are so hot!" Hot is the beauty code word for Type 3 women.

True to your fiery nature that comes from your dominant element hydrogen, it just makes sense that when *Dressing Your Truth®* you look hot! And this beauty code word does not just apply to younger Type 3 women. I have seen many Type 3 women over 55 go from looking quite grandmotherly to looking hot after their transformation!

I have heard some Type 3 women who are hesitant to dress their truth in fear of looking too sexy and hot. They have been trying to tone down their more substantial nature for many years, and to step into their truth and look sexy, hot and amazing can be quite a step for some women. Let yourself come back to your truth as a Type 3 woman, fully embracing and loving your new hot and sexy look!

YOUR BEAUTY SIXTH SENSE
DRESSING YOUR TRUTH TIP

You are a determined woman and you don't like to fuss over yourself. You need to honor your desire to accomplish your tasks swiftly and practically. Saving money and saving time while looking great is your nature. Honor this natural movement of yours by shopping sales and shopping in spurts. Make sure you have a no-fuss hairstyle that can look great in 10 to 20 minutes. If it takes you more time than that, you will not be interested in keeping it that style very long! Honor your beauty sixth sense by maintaining your swift, no-fuss, practical nature. Learning to Dress Your Truth will give you the tools to do this and look amazing everyday of your life.

Don't let your practical nature keep you from investing in our *Dressing Your Truth*® online experience. I have seen too many Type 3s think they know what they are doing and they charge ahead trying to dress their truth only to guess their truth! They end up wasting more money, wishing they had taken the time to learn how to truly dress their truth!

Remember, I am a Type 3! I know our tendencies!

FAMOUS TYPE 3 WOMEN

Mary J. Blige, Cindy Crawford, Amelia Earhart, Whoopi Goldberg, Katharine Hepburn, Beyonce Knowles, Eva Mendes, Michelle Obama, Susan Sarandon, Shakira, Maria Shriver, Hilary Swank, Taylor Swift, Tina Turner, Barbara Walters, Raquel Welch, Serena Williams, and Oprah Winfrey.

KAY'S STORY

Kay used to focus on what she thought was wrong with her. Growing up, she always tried to be like her big sister—the one who was the beauty queen, the star soprano in chorus, the favorite babysitter of all the neighbors. She was even valedictorian of her high school.

Kay looked totally different than her sister did. Kay's sister had skin that would tan, had a small waist and very feminine hands, but Kay had freckles and red hair, a boyish figure, and more masculine hands. Kay's face was also more angular with a high forehead. She was always trying to hide her so-called flaws.

"I used to feel almost apologetic for being competitive and driven," Kay says. "I thought I was that way, in part, because I was always trying to match up to my big sister. My friends would tell me I was working too hard, and to sit back and smell the roses."

Kay currently has two businesses, and loves them both. Even so, up until now, she always felt that she had to make excuses for being so driven. She can't stand sitting around doing nothing, and for many years she thought she had some sort of psychological hang up.

When she discovered that she is a Type 3 Woman, she was happy to find that Type 3s love action! They also do well in business and make good leaders. And even their physical characteristics are strong or what Kay used to call masculine.

"I finally felt it's okay to be me, just the way I am!" Kay says happily now. "My friends have noticed that I assert myself more now. Where before I would go along with whatever restaurant or movie just to please them, now I state what I really want. I feel so much happier now. No more feeling like I have to hide myself or my true feelings."

DIANE'S STORY

For this last Type 3 story, I will let Diane tell it herself. "When I attended a Dressing Your Truth® training, I was very interested in what you had to say! I had studied color analysis 25 years ago, and actually sold make-up and color draped people. We did it in seasons way back then, and I was pegged as a vibrant summer. I have spent the last 25 years wearing vibrant, cool colors and only silver jewelry. You can guess what my initial reaction was to finding out that I am a dominant Type 3 woman. I started to tremble inside and couldn't imagine that I was supposed to be that dynamic, warm woman.

"Well, as I took time and really searched inside, I started to remember the assertive girl that I was in college, and how I enjoyed people and being involved with lots of things.

"Going to the Dressing Your Truth® event started awareness inside me and got me so excited I felt like I was going to burst. I wanted to know more and I wanted it now (so Type 3, right?)

"I needed my hair colored and cut anyway, so I couldn't wait to come and have your Dressing Your Truth® hair stylist give me some advice as to how my hair would best fit me. I was very nervous, but let her do it. And I loved it! I feel like a new woman and feel like I am starting to be who I was meant to be again.

"My family is in awe. As I go to church and run into friends, they are all wowed with my new look. I think, as much as I have a new look on the outside, I feel different inside. I carry myself differently and feel younger and lighter.

"This process has been great for my soul, my family and those around me. My hubby loves my shift and notices that I am changing. I have several people interested in Dressing your Truth because I have shared with them how much that one event started my life change. Thank you for the fun new journey."

SUMMARY OF THE TYPE 3
RICH, DYNAMIC WOMAN

Hydrogen/fire is Type 3 energy. A Type 3 has an active/reactive energy. You are a results-oriented, passionate person. Your dominant shape in physical features is the triangle and this is visible in the eyebrows, eyes and cheeks and overall facial shape.

As a Type 3 woman you may have a tendency toward these strengths:

- You are a radiant source of movement and energy—a fireball.

- You are action oriented with a driving force to accomplish or compete.

- You have an abundance of sureness about moving forward, and you inspire others to have confidence in you, even if you don't feel confident.

- You have the capacity to accomplish big things in a big way. You think big.

- You are an entrepreneur by nature and can easily figure out ways to make money doing what you like to do.

- You are a natural salesperson. You know how to promote and bring in the buyer. And you also know how to close the deal.

- You are an independent soul and do not need approval from others to move forward.

- You are decisive and can easily "take the ball and run with it."

- You are task-oriented and can solve problems and get results very quickly.

- You are deliberate and to the point in all that you do.

As a Type 3 you may have a tendency towards these weaknesses:

- You may be too pushy, too aggressive, too bossy or too abrupt for other Types.

- You may be inconsiderate of other people's feelings when you're on a path to accomplish something and they get in your way.

- You may be moving forward so quickly that you don't take enough time to get the details.

- You may think that it has to fit your way of doing it or it's just nonsense.

TYPE 3 BEAUTY KEY WORDS

Active	Ornate
Adventurous	Outgoing
Ambitious	Outstanding
Angled	Positive
Assured	Powerful
Asymmetrical	Practical
Big Hearted	Purposeful
Captivating	Quick
Casual	Resourceful
Confident	Richness
Daring	Rough
Dashing	Rugged Rustic
Dazzling	Self-confident
Dynamic	Sharp
Earthy	Showy
Eloquent	Social
Energetic	Solid
Exciting	Spicy
Exotic	Spirited
Expressive	Strong
Fiery	Substantial
Flamboyant	Sultry
Glowing	Sure
High-spirited	Swift
Hot	Tawny
Independent	Tenacious
Industrious	Textured
Informal	To the point
Intense	Unevenness
Inventive	Vigorous
Lavish	Vitality
Lustrous	Vivid
Magnetic	Voluptuous
Mover and Shaker	Warmth
No frills	Wild
No fuss	Zesty

TYPE 4: THE BOLD, STRIKING WOMAN

Primary Movement: *Constant, Still*

Natural Gift: *Perfecting—"Here is how we can make it better, and here is how we can duplicate it."*

Dominant Quality: *Serenely reflecting truth back to us and improving the quality of our lives.*

Beauty Code Word: *Stunning!*

THE TYPE 4 EXPRESSION COMES FROM THE ELEMENT OF CARBON/ EARTH, and its natural primary movement is constant and still. If you have a dominant Type 4 movement, you have a constant, exact energy. You are reflective, concise and clear. The dominant shapes in your physical features are elongated ovals with straight sides, parallel lines in any direction, which are visible in the eyes, the nose, the cheeks, the hairline, and overall body and facial shape.

Type 4 energy is an introvert expression reflecting perfection to create in this world. As a Type 4, you express a low level to almost no movement. This keen, precise, still movement can be consistently observed through aspects of your human experience.

Other key words that describe the movement of this energy in a dominant Type 4 woman are: bold, authoritative, keen, regal, polished, striking, sleek, structured, clean, clear, simple, reflective, exact and grounding.

Due to your low-to-no-movement that expresses itself as solid and structured, you may have been told a lot as a child, and even in your adult life, to "Lighten up!" or "Don't be so literal or critical!" or "You're always so serious."

Your energy has the firm and statuesque presence of a noble fir tree or the reflective quality of a still lake mirroring perfection back to the world.

Keeping things structured and staying on track is the primary motive for a Type 4 woman. Creating quality and precision is a priority in how you approach life. The movement of Type 4 Energy is the most rigid of all the Types. For this reason I have noticed that, of all the Types, Type 4 is the most misunderstood and can be the most misjudged and unappreciated. Others tend to perceive this energy as too authoritative, too critical, and overly serious. Understanding this movement gives us the opportunity to understand your Type 4 nature with more respect and honor for the gift and talent you so beautifully bring to the whole.

I have the great blessing of currently having three dominant Type 4 members in our family—my son Mark, my son-in-law Tony, and my grandson Seth. I started to develop this information when my son Mark (Type 4) was about 16 years old. Understanding the dynamics of his natural, core movement, and how it is expressing itself through so many aspects of his life, has been one of the most valuable insights I could ever hope for as his mother. Being able to honor and understand his constant still nature, and what that looks like in his everyday tendencies as a person, has allowed me to see and experience his truth, and to respect and honor him deeply when the exact same tendencies could have easily been misunderstood as negative personality traits by me.

Because I don't have a Type 4 female in my family, I will be referring to a few personal experiences with the male members of my family, and also Type 4 females I have known and worked with, to help you better understand the nature of a Type 4.

126

If you are a Type 4, it is not typical that you look to outside sources to help you understand yourself better. One of your tendencies is to be deeply reflective, and to pride yourself in just naturally knowing who you are. I can see why you would consider a system that does not recognize this as a waste of your time. The *Beauty Profiling*^{SM} system, on the other hand, truly recognizes you and honors who you are.

As a Type 4, you like to play by the rules as long as you can trust the source of those rules or the rules themselves. Once you respect and accept the authority of another person or an organization, the rules they lay down are easier for you to accept and keep, even if you do not fully agree with those rules. More than following rules, a Type 4 also likes to create rules for others to follow.

I recognize you to be the authority in your own world. I offer you this *Beauty Profile*^{SM} model as an opportunity to add to your already clear understanding of who you are and what is important to you.

I have learned that you generally don't like being told what Type you are, especially if you are a Type 4. I don't believe it is my role to tell you precisely what Type you are. You will know it innately, after some guidance. No two people are exactly alike but I think you will agree with me that even you, as a Type 4, will find some uncanny similarities that you will recognize in yourself and others as you read through this section.

My hope for you is that you will allow yourself to use this information to add quality to your relationships and your life.

Let me illustrate that with a comment I heard not long ago. At a recent Profiling class, a woman who was a Type 4 came up to me after the end of the class and shared with me, "I believe this information could have helped me turn my marriage around before we divorced."

Type 4 and Type 3 energies are very bold expressions of energy. Notably, you have not been considered feminine in your nature in our culture of the past. This can be especially challenging for a woman who is a dominant Type 4. I am grateful to offer this information to help women live their truth and express their bold, striking nature!

=====

JEAN'S STORY

Learning her true Profile has resulted in profound changes in Jean's life. Her profile revealed that she was exactly what she thought she wasn't, and she had a hard time accepting it as she had strong judgments on myself and her way of being.

"I was living primarily in my secondary Type," Jean confesses, "always wanting to be something completely different—hiding out and not feeling authentic. I could never put my finger on why."

Learning her Type brought clarity to her gifts and had such a grounding effect on her. She was finally comfortable being quiet and contemplative in the company of others, finally appreciating her ability to see things with a critical eye as a gift, not a fault. She has also become more willing to say things directly, rather than beating around the bush to be nice out of fear of judgment.

This shift for her has created shifts in many of her relationships—some ending, some new ones forming, some deepening—but in all of them, she feels more true to herself and a deeper and better appreciation of others, especially her family. Her new knowledge has been a springboard for new possibilities in her life—reigniting a fresh spirit within her.

"I feel strong and hopeful, and blessed to have been so validated by learning this information!"

=====

128

NATURAL GIFTS AND TALENTS

Type 4s complete our cycle of wholeness. To recap, Type 1s start the cycle by initiating an idea with the hope it can be done; Type 2s gather the details to make the plan; Type 3s push us into action to create a result; and Type 4s have a keen awareness to step back and analyze the whole process and consider what has been created to see how it can be improved.

If you were to put your natural gift into a phrase, your phrase would be, "Here is how we can make it better, and here is how we can duplicate it."

You truly see the world through a critical eye with a desire for perfecting things around you. Because of your reflective quality, you not only want to perfect the world, you want to share what you believe, which brings quality to our lives by duplicating it.

Type 4s step back from a situation rather than jumping into it. This allows you to take in the bigger picture and see what is going on.

Your keen eye and gift of precision helps you see all the pieces and how they fit together to create a perfect whole. You have the gift of being able to make anything more perfect and systemize any process to a desired, repeatable and predictable outcome. You take things to their final perfected form.

Your primary shape is reflecting, parallel lines. You can see the straight line in your movement from point A to point B. You move through life by taking the most direct, straightforward route, once you have determined the exact goal. One of your dominant shapes in your facial features (such as the bridge of your nose) is parallel lines moving in any direction—horizontal, vertical, and a fast diagonal line.

You have a naturally keen view of your world. When you feel inspired, you share your awareness in a very concise manner. You can't help that what you first see in something or some situation is what is weak or at fault. You may not always share this insight, but you will always lead with those thoughts.

Important: It is important as a Type 4 that you acknowledge yourself to be precise and structured. If you try to lighten up your movement and become more random and animated, your 4-ness will bleed through and that can shock people!

When you do not allow your Dominant Type to lead in your expressive self, you lose your connection with who you are. You will be out of balance from your constant, still energy if you try to force yourself to lighten up and animate yourself. You are not able to fake how you feel.

My son Mark (Type 4) admits that he cannot force and fake his feelings. For example, if he were to be given a gift for his birthday that he does not feel excited about, he can politely receive and appreciate it but he can't fake being excited about it. It's just not available to him in his movement.

In 2008, the hit Broadway play *Mama Mia* became a popular movie starring Meryl Streep (Type 1) and Pierce Brosnan (Type 4). Meryl Streep, due to her naturally animated nature, shined in the movie. Pierce Brosnan, due to his naturally still nature, came off rigid and stiff in the singing and dancing scenes.

Another amazing gift you share with humanity is your energetic gift of reflecting truth back to others. When you are living in harmony with your true nature, you naturally reflect the truth of others back to them. You are an energetic mirror for others, sending the silent message, "Be true to yourself and believe in yourself." There is nothing you actually have to do—just being present offers this gift.

The same natural tendencies that are your gifts and talents can also be a challenge in your life, causing temporary imbalance and disharmony. While you always lead with your Dominant Type, when your dominant movement is taking over your life and is not balanced with the other three Types (which are also a part of your being), it can be a challenge being you!

Challenge: You may appear harsh, judgmental or too opinionated. Because you have a tendency to see weakness first, you can come across as critical and negative. Knowing this about yourself, you can manage your gift with more awareness and choose how you express your insights in a manner that does not appear overly critical. You may have even tried to become less judgmental, less critical, and less negative because you have been told too often that these are purely negative attributes. However, it is impossible to eliminate your gifts of discernment because you cannot change your inner nature. It is your blueprint.

PERSONALITY TRAITS

You are your own authority. You do not give that authority to others but will look to others you perceive as an authority—in their expertise in life—to guide you in your interests. If you perceive their authority as trustworthy, you will follow their guidance and rules; if you do not trust their authority, you may abide by their rules for a time only to get to someplace you want to go. If someone tries to be an uninvited authority over you, you think in your mind, "I didn't ask you to tell me what to do or how to do it." You would especially not welcome to this kind of authority if it comes from someone you viewed to have no more authority over a topic or situation that you.

You look at what has been created with a critical eye, then evaluate and determine what could be done better. Type 4s have a keen focus so you stay on course easily. You also demand perfection and want things to be the best they can be. As a Type 4, you expect the best from others and hold a high standard. You move forward with crystal clear, focused determination while maintaining a quiet confidence that you can do it better than most people.

Your native element is carbon/earth. Phrases used to describe your personality are: "You are such a pillar of strength." Or when it becomes a judgment, "You take things too seriously or literally!"

You do not like being put in the limelight spontaneously; however, when you choose it, you are very effective in influencing others.

For example, it was my son Mark's (Type 4) birthday. He came home from school that day and I asked him how his day had been. He replied, "It was the worst day of my life!" I asked him why and he shared, "I walked into the lunch room and all my friends started singing 'Happy Birthday' to me in front of everyone! I turned around and walked out because it was so uncomfortable for me."

The irony in this quality is that you are the most striking women in the world, and though you may prefer to go unnoticed, you can't help but stand out, especially when you are *Dressing Your Truth*®.

At our *Dressing Your Truth*® events, we see some of the most remarkable transformations occur with the Type 4 women. Often, they don't especially stand out when the event starts. By the end of the training, they are some of the most noticeable individuals in the room. They are striking and immediately stand out due to their naturally stunning appearance. You need to recognize that even though you may not want a lot of attention drawn to you, your stunning looks naturally get the attention of others. You will find that the kind of attention you get at *Dressing Your Truth*® events will be respectful, the kind of attention you enjoy.

Challenge: Your presence of authority and boldness can unknowingly come across as intimidating to others. You may have been judging this quality as negative and trying to lighten or soften yourself. An easier way to deal with this quality is to realize that others are giving you unspoken authority to initiate interaction with them. You would actually prefer it this way as you are not fond of random interactions at the whim of others. You prefer to choose who you would like to interact with and who you invite into your personal space.

Challenge: You can get stuck by wanting every little part and piece perfect. You demand too much of yourself and others, and you don't want to get off track. You need to learn to say "It's good enough" and move on. Rather than try to perfect everything, channel your gift into what truly is important to you and adds quality to your life and to the lives of those you love. Then let those things that aren't that important to you just be good enough.

Challenge: More than any other Type, you will find it harder to change your direction when things are not working out, especially if they were well planned in the first place. As a Type 4, you may even find it hard to stop reading a book that you started, even if you don't like it!

You are private, disciplined, influential and uncompromising in your approach to life. It will suit you to have an agreed upon starting time and finishing time for your leisure time. Within this structure, you can really let your focus go, knowing there will be a time you will get back on track with the non-leisure time activities in your life.

Challenge: Due to your gift of perfecting things, you have a tendency to set standards that neither you nor anyone else can meet. This can set you up to feel that you can never fulfill your desired expectations, and always fall short of the mark. With your tendency towards perfection, you can create low self-esteem and pessimism in your view of yourself, others and life in general.

Challenge: You steer away from things that you cannot easily be perfect in. Your tendency for high expectations can place a great demand on yourself, and you may be limiting your interests and opportunity to try new things due to your perfecting nature.

THOUGHT AND FEELING PROCESSES

Your thoughts and feelings are deep and reflective, far reaching and penetrating. You are not satisfied with the superficial. You search for the cause and correlation of things, seeking to understand the laws that affect human life. You are a clear thinker and a thorough and efficient organizer of your thoughts. It is important for you to mentally organize your thoughts so you can move forward within a framework of structure. You are not at ease until this state has been achieved. You take in a lot of information and can quickly figure out what has value to you and what does not.

You really have a very soft-hearted disposition. You reveal your innermost thoughts and feelings reluctantly and only to those whom you trust. Your feelings are deep and tender. You easily empathize with others and have the ability to make very deep commitments.

Challenge: In your tendency to think in black and white terms, you can be an all-or-nothing thinker.

Challenge: You can become deeply focused and often tense, but focusing on a project or activity can also help you relax.

Challenge: When you are emotionally triggered, your energy can be read as icy or cool, just like an icicle or an iceberg—cold and immovable.

Challenge: You can be labeled a "know it all." This is an accurate description of you, however, because your keenness and concise way of thinking does offer you the gift of knowing better than most about a lot of things!

COMMUNICATION

You value respect, loyalty, reliability, professionalism, appropriate humor, and timeliness in your communication with others.

You do not like being put on the spot spontaneously but are eager to express yourself before a group if you have some purpose in view. You have a gift of being concise in your communication, and are able to share a lot of information clearly and in a few words. You are brief but comprehensive.

You are quiet about your thoughts until you are clear about how you feel. When you are clear, you form strong opinions about what is right or wrong, having a black and white opinion, with no gray areas. You may not always share your keen insight and strong opinions. It depends on how worthy you feel your listening audience is.

When you have engaged in a conversation with another person, you give them your full attention and expect to be given the same when sharing your thoughts and feelings. You do not like being interrupted in the middle of sharing your stream of thought. It is especially irritating to be interrupted if you are intensely focused on a project or activity while someone tries to talk to you and interrupts you.

I have learned, for example, that it is difficult for my son Mark (Type 4) to give me his attention when he is concentrating on his computer, homework, mountain bikes, or any other activity he is focused on. If I try to engage him in a conversation spontaneously, I will most likely not receive a response. If I keep persisting and push him to respond to me, he has a tendency to get upset and snap at me. A choice that is more honorable is to ask him something like, "When can I talk to you?" Then together we create the structure he needs to shift tracks and give his full attention when the time is right for him.

When asked a question, you expect the person who asked the question to pay attention to your answer. If the person doesn't pay close attention to your answer, and asks the question again, the question seems redundant and superficial to you because you don't like to repeat yourself. You give your full attention to others and expect them to respond in kind when engaging in conversation with you.

Challenge: You may sound critical or overly negative to others. You like to get to the essence as quickly as possible, and you can come across as blunt and too straightforward in expressing your opinions.

Challenge: You can be too authoritative, bossy or condescending.

Challenge: You may build walls around yourself so others cannot approach you, and they won't know how to talk to you.

BEHAVIORAL TENDENCIES

You express yourself in a straightforward manner. You like to get to the bottom line as soon as you can. You tend to stay on track, even when you move between tracks, or from one activity to another.

RELATIONSHIPS—You are a loyal and faithful friend, true to your word. If you make a promise, you keep it. It is your tendency to be self-sacrificing for the people with whom you are the closest. The more you feel you are being honored, the more easily you make who you are available to others, and even yourself.

Challenge: You may be cold and distant, content to live in your own world as this mode feels less painful to you if you have felt misunderstood.

SOCIAL—You do not form acquaintances readily. You are not the one who will be chatting with the person next to you in the grocery line; in fact, you probably think it does not make sense to do so when you don't even know the person! Rather, you prefer a narrow range of friends to whom you are very close and loyal. Even though you don't like to be in the spotlight, your striking presence draws unwelcome attention to you.

TIMELINESS—You are always on time, or early. Of the four Energy Types, you have the greatest tendency for timeliness. You take things literally and when someone says I will meet you at 4 o'clock, 4 o'clock means 4 o'clock. You take it personally and feel dishonored when the people you are closest to are consistently late.

Not long after my daughter Jenny (Type 1) and Tony (Type 4) were newly married, Tony started medical school. Tony was taking the bus and Jenny was picking him up at the agreed upon time of 5:00 PM. In Jenny's words, "I would consistently get there late every day. I was thinking that it was no big deal to be a little late. I really believed my timing was close enough." This happened for several weeks. One day she was 45 minutes late and things were getting tense. Tony finally had to talk about it. Tony shared with Jenny that it would mean a lot to him for her to be on time. "When we agreed on 5 o'clock, I expect you to be here at 5 o'clock." The bottom line for Tony was Jenny wasn't keeping her word, and it was personally offensive to Tony. Jenny admitted she was embarrassed and didn't want to admit that she had dropped the ball so many times. "Once I realized how important it was for Tony and how important exactness and keeping your word was to him, I committed to always be on time," which she has done. This also demonstrates one valid motivation for conforming to the needs of others: the intent to honor another's Type.

WORK—You will thrive the most in a position that allows you to be your own authority. You have a natural tendency to stay on track with your work and to mentally organize yourself in such a way that you do not need an authority watching over you or micro-managing you. You quickly see what needs to be done and how to do it better than most.

When my son Mark (Type 4) was 17 years old, he started a successful eBay business selling used mountain bikes. I helped him learn how to set up and run an eBay business. He quickly learned what he needed to do to make it successful. He thoroughly enjoyed being his own boss.

One afternoon, I asked him if he was keeping accounting records of his sales and tracking his profits. He looked at me somewhat irritated and said, "No, mom, I am stupid. I am not doing any of that!" Of course, he was. He's a Type 4! He definitely was blunt with me, yet understanding his Type 4 tendencies in his response, I did not take it personally. I simply responded, "Okay, that was blunt! My intention was to support you and see if you needed any help with that. I apologize if how I asked made you assume that you didn't know what you were doing. Let me rephrase that: 'Is there anything I can help you with in your business, Mark?'" I also encouraged him to work on his tendency to be overly blunt and speak more respectfully, which he agreed to do. We both learned more about how to communicate effectively in honoring our very different natural tendencies.

MONEY—You are very thorough in how you plan your spending. You tend to think things through before you spend your money. You prefer to save your money so you can invest in the best of what you want. You prefer to own less, but what you own needs to be of good quality and of value to you.

PHYSICAL ACTIVITY—You enjoy activities that require your ability to focus intensely and perfect your physical talents. You enjoy single sports and recreational pursuits. It makes sense that my Type 4 son-in-law Tony loves to rock climb. It is intense, requires great focus and one must be very thorough in the preparation and execution of the sport.

A physical activity that you have a unique tendency with is your experience of driving. You think you are the best driver on the road. It bothers you that others don't understand and follow the rules of driving as well as you do. Your Type 4 tendencies can really manifest when you are driving because you notice what you perceive as the weaknesses of other drivers. You are not shy about sharing how you feel about such weaknesses, in a blunt, opinionated way.

Another tendency I have noticed that is unique to your still and reflective nature is that you do not like to be rubbed or patted on your body in the same place over and over. You prefer a firm strong hug from a loved one over being continually stroked or patted.

BODY LANGUAGE

Not all of your body language and physical features will express themselves in a Type 4 movement. Most women are blended in their physical features, so you won't see yourself in all these expressions, but you will notice that you have many expressions of body language and physical features that are Type 4 if you are a dominant Type 4 woman.

WALKING—You walk with little movement of your limbs and body in a very upright, still, stately manner.

SITTING/STANDING—You sit very upright, with straight posture, both feet on the ground, hands folded or hanging on sides. Your sitting and standing could be called proper with a formal look. Most runway models are dominant Type 4s— naturally erect, poised, and structured in movement with straight shoulders and perfect posture—striking, of course.

VOICE/LANGUAGE—A Type 4 voice is a lower pitch, with a clear, clean, smooth sound. You speak little but with a clear intent, using bold language. You say it how it is, just like Simon Cowell (Type 4) on American Idol. Favorite words that you use frequently in your verbal expressions are: exactly, definitely, precisely, or perfect. You use phrases like, "That was stupid!" or "The meeting started at 11 o'clock, not 11:02." People who do voiceover work can tend to be Type 4 as their voices are clear, precise, bold voices.

DOODLING— You do not have a tendency to doodle—it's just too much movement. However, rather than doodling, you do tend to edit writing, noticing when things are misspelled or grammatically incorrect.

PERSONAL SPACE—You like to keep things put away and out of sight, creating empty or negative space with no movement. You like your space to be clean, clear and orderly.

INTERIOR DESIGN—Type 4 movement in interior design is what we call modern and contemporary. The design is simple and sleek with bold structures and décor.

KALISTA'S STORY

Throughout her life, Kalista has not enjoyed social situations. She always felt like she had to force herself to be pleasant and make conversation. Her parents tried to help her overcome this problem with even more social activities. She would try to be fun, but it felt fake and gave her anxiety.

"Your Profiling system made me face my true self," Kalista admits. "I cried myself to sleep that first night after learning my Type. I felt like all those feelings and labels of 'too picky, cold, unsocial, shy, quiet, critical' were confirmed."

Her husband felt at first like she was being put in a box. It was only after a few days of reflection and facing her "stuff" before she began to see the beauty and complex nature of a Type 4. It was not just okay to be still, it was perfect for her! This gift has allowed her to love herself, the part of herself that is constant, still, bold, precise.

Kalista now reports that her interactions with others are more enjoyable, now that she is not trying to be what she thought others wanted out of her. "I live an authentic expression now," she says. "Others see that and get me for who I am. Understanding my truth lets others experience me in a way that is harmonious, honest and honoring."

PHYSICAL FEATURES

The overall quality of your expression is sculpted, striking and symmetrical. Your bone structure creates parallel lines and elongated ovals. For visual examples and pictures of Type 4 facial features, please watch the Type 4 *Beauty Profile*SM course at www.dressingyourtruth.com.

SKIN AND SKIN TEXTURE—Type 4 skin is clear and reflective which gives it a porcelain, striking quality, with minimal lines and small pores. This is due to the stillness in their being, which expresses itself as very small pores in their skin. Many models featured in skin care product commercials have Type 4 skin. However, it is not the skincare product that is creating their porcelain skin: it is their stillness that expresses itself as small pores.

FACE SHAPE—Elongated oval, or rectangular with parallel lines on sides of face and across hairline. A broad forehead. A widows peak is a Type 4 feature as it creates a point that divides the face into a mirror image of itself. The actress Courteney Cox is a good example of this. You could take one side of her face, and it would mirror perfectly the exact same features on the other side of her face.

CHEEKS—Fast parallel lines, what we call high cheek bones, oval shaped.

NOSE—Two straight lines on side of nose bridge, sideways oval between nostrils, oval nostrils, and straight nose bridge.

EYEBROWS—Straight lines, or half of elongated oval.

EYES—Oval, bold, reflective, straight line along the bottom of the eyelid.

HANDS—Very smooth, porcelain skin on top of the palm; parallel lines on sides of fingers; parallel lines on sides of nail beds, long fingers, often the same width all the way down the finger, creating parallel lines.

HOW YOUR ENERGY AFFECTS OTHER PEOPLE

Your energy creates an ambience of clearness and stability. Your constant, still energy quiets the people around you. You are naturally a stabilizing force to the rest of us. When you feel like other people are cool to you, what is really occurring is their demeanor is showing respect for the authoritative, reflective qualities you emanate.

Because others feel that you are unapproachable, it would be smart for you to know that it works well for you to initiate interaction with others. When you are uncomfortable or disturbed, you move into a state of more stillness and your constant still energy can come across to other Energy Types as cool and distant.

As you are conscious of your natural movement and are more aware of others, you will be able to manage yourself in a way that supports them in being in rapport with you. As you stay conscious of and love who you are, rather than judge your natural movement, you will be consistently aligned with your core true nature. Others will be more likely to enjoy being around you.

Now I'll explore some specifics around fashion and a Type 4 woman.

SENDING THE RIGHT MESSAGE: HOW YOUR APPEARANCE AFFECTS OTHER PEOPLE

When you don't dress your truth, you send a message that conflicts with who you truly are. Your nature is to be bold and authoritative. When you wear clothes that make you appear soft and subtle, your nature will be disguised to most others, and you can often be judged as too sever and even rigid. Type 4 women often think, "If I dress more bold and striking, I will come across intimidating." This is not the case! When you dress your truth, your inner truth is in harmony with your outer appearance, and you will be taken seriously for who you are: a bold, striking woman.

What you are wearing sends a message to other people which influences their first impression of you. If you don't dress your truth, you may be judged in a negative light because your true nature is not being honored by your appearance. You have a gift of bringing exactness and order to any situation. Set the mood everywhere you go by dressing your truth and letting your gift of strength and confidence be expressed in your outer appearance.

MOST COMMON FASHION MISTAKES

It is common for a Type 4 woman to try and subdue her very bold, authoritative nature by wearing soft, flowing clothes. Softened fabrication only conflicts with who you are. When your bold, blunt, clear expression comes out naturally, you will be perceived as too blunt, too serious and too authoritative. Softened fabrications also make you appear frumpy. I have seen many Type 4s turn from frumpy to stunning. It is quite a sight to behold! ! To watch a Type 4 makeover showing how a Type 4 woman can go from

143

frumpy to stunning, please visit the Type 4 makeover on www. thecarolblog.com.

SHOPPING TENDENCIES

Your exact nature lends itself to your clothes and the way they fit. More than any Type, you are very keenly aware of the fit of a garment. You demand perfection in the way your clothes fit on your body, even to the point of taking them to a tailor to get the exact fit that feels right to you. You may be perceived as "too picky." It's just your tendency: you look for perfection and don't like to settle for less.

You prefer to find one-of-a-kind clothes that make your look unique. You stay away from the trendiest clothing and styles, not wanting to look like every other woman.

You are so against over-worked trends that if *Dressing Your Truth*® becomes a "trend" you may hesitate to join the club. You seek to keep your unique, individual style. You can learn the basic components of *Dressing Your Truth*® and make them your own. I'm confident you will love *Dressing Your Truth*® as it speaks to your true nature. Your keen instincts may already be present in your shopping traits. It will just make knowing what is right for you more clear and exact in your mind.

Tamara shares this about her shopping tendencies as a Type 4: "You know us so well, Carol. I love tailored clothes that feel as though they are hugging me. I also know (and feel) as soon as I put something on whether it is right for me (it has to be a perfect fit, especially shoes). And when they do fit, I feel they were made just for me! I am also guilty of wanting one-of-a-kind clothes. I don't like having the same clothes everybody else has or shopping where everyone else does. I like one-of-a-kind clothes because I am one of a kind and why not dress to support that?"

You may find that you have a tendency to make rules to shop by. You actually make a lot of rules for yourself that you live by unconsciously. Shauna shares the following experience about her personal shopping rules.

"I would rather deal with clothes I have than to shop to find new clothes because I know exactly what I want, and do not have a difficult time finding what I want.... I have the best success shopping alone, and, yes, I search to find the perfect one-of-a-kind item. I very rarely have clothing similar to someone else's. If I do end up with a "twin," I usually send it to charity. I have many rules about clothing!"

THE TYPE 4 WOMAN BEAUTY CODE WORD

Every woman is remarkably beautiful, no matter what Type she is. Your natural feminine expression lends itself for you to have a certain kind of beauty that depicts what Type of woman you are. When Dressing Your truth and honoring your truest beauty, a Type 4 woman will be told often, "You are stunning!" Stunning is the beauty code word for the Type 4 woman.

You truly are a stunning beauty that others have a hard time not staring at in awe. Type 4 beauty is the beauty of the fashion world. It has become the standard of beauty that too many women compare themselves to. Nearly every fashion model is a dominant Type 4 woman, or has a very strong secondary Type 4 in their physical features. When women like Brooke Shields, Cindy Crawford and Christie Brinkley become the standard of what beauty is, only other Type 4 women have a chance at achieving this stunning beauty!

Take it upon yourself to bring out your bold, striking, stunning beauty and to honor yourself and share with others. Even though you do not like being the center of attention, you will enjoy standing out in a crowd in a way that you are perceived as a unique woman who truly knows who she is and where she is going in life.

YOUR BEAUTY SIXTH SENSE DRESSING YOUR TRUTH TIP

You have a natural gift for structure and order in your life. Your exact nature needs to be honored in how you dress and accessorize. You are very aware of how a garment fits on your body and prefer to have an exact fit. If what you are putting on your body does not fit you exactly according to your specifications, you will not be drawn to wearing it. If you have compromised on this, these are the garments that hang ignored in your closet. You will always choose to wear the clothes that fit you more perfectly. Honor your beauty sixth sense and make sure what you buy fits you exactly how you want it to, or make sure you can take it to a tailor to get that fit!

FAMOUS TYPE 4 WOMEN

Halle Berry, Victoria Beckham, Courteney Cox, Megan Fox, Anne Hathaway, Audrey Hepburn, Heidi Klum, Keira Knightley, Lucy Liu, Demi Moore, Jackie Onassis, Gwyneth Paltrow, Jada Pinkett-Smith, Natalie Portman, Zoe Saldana, Gwen Stefani, Kristen Stewart, Elizabeth Taylor, Liv Tyler, and Twiggy (Lesley Hornby).

SHERYL'S STORY

Another Type 4 story is Sheryl's. It's fascinating. I'll let her tell it to you herself.

"As a woman and the CEO of an international company, I was extremely frustrated by the treatment I often received, not just from men but also from women I met in association with our business. Rather than talking with me, they so often requested that they please talk with my husband, who was my partner. They couldn't imagine that I was actually the CEO. My talented husband and I had divided our duties, but I really did oversee everything. However, I was often ignored or insulted by associates in our industry, and I admit that

sometimes I chose to return an abrasive chain of words. That reaction certainly didn't help! Here I was, a sweet, mousy, frumpy person telling them bluntly how I felt, and they didn't expect it out of me nor did they like it.

"*When situations like that happened, I was so mad at myself for not being more flexible and kind. I hated the part of me that was so headstrong. Why couldn't I just be nice all of the time? So I tried the other path and when people insulted me or treated me poorly, I bit my tongue and stuffed my opinions and my anger. That caused havoc with my health, my marriage, and my happiness.*

"*When I met Carol, I was trying to be perfect at being everything Type 2 energy is. Problem was, I absolutely could not do it. I felt like a failure. After I studied each Type and understood more fully what Type 2 energy was, I knew without a doubt that it wasn't me. That was actually a huge relief. I was now on an adventure to find out who I really was.*

"*I attended one of Carol's events, and she brought the entire group of Type 1 energy people together at the front of the audience. My sister was one of them! I was envious and wanted to be in that group, with the bouncy, entertaining, laughing, quick-witted people. But as much as I love that energy, I knew right away it wasn't in my nature to be like that. So I thought I must be a Type 3. I get things done! I'm opinionated! But Carol wasn't convinced.*

"*I didn't even consider Type 4 energy—it was perfectionist and judgmental and I thought that must be bad. But the more I studied what Type 4 energy was, the more I began to see it in myself—the perfect way to load a dishwasher, the way I lined up my socks into columns and colors in my drawer, seeing the big picture, seeing people's potential, judgments that I placed on others, and, most especially, on myself, plus the way I liked to be alone sometimes. The way I sat completely straight. And, okay, my stubbornness.*

"*And the stillness I had, even as a child. When I was two years old, I sat on the bottom shelf in a store right among the life-sized dolls, wearing my fashionable winter coat and hat. A lady shopper was examining all of the dolls carefully, deciding which to buy. I sat there very still, but when she got close enough to touch me, I jumped up and ran away. She screamed!*

"After contemplating all of this, I was hit by the brightest and most wonderful light! I had a dominant Type 4 energy! It was the most freeing, amazing, lifting feeling I had ever known.

"I love knowing who I am! Now I understand why I think, walk, talk and act the way I do. And guess what? It's okay! It's fabulous! Now I can enter a room or stand at a trade show and I receive respect. Why? I think it's because I am living more closely to the way I was made to be. People seem to be aware that I know what I want and I am rarely ignored or insulted. That frees me up and allows me to actually be more kind.

"I'm not turning cartwheels to try to get my way. I don't have to be abrasive because I have learned to use my energy without even speaking. Somehow, others know who I am—my energy conveys it. Now that I have learned about my weaknesses, I've worked dili-gently to not be so hard on others and on myself. And I don't have to be right. I now know how to better approach my children and husband. I am also better at communicating with our customers. And I have strengths! My opinions are strong, and that's great! I have an incredible sense of direction or gut feeling when it comes to making business decisions. I've helped improve our products and that brings me great joy! I feel and think deeply.

"I went from loathing myself for not being what I thought I should be, to accepting and loving myself for what I am and what I have to offer. Basically, I've learned that I'm okay, and that's made a world of difference. Thanks, Carol Tuttle! You have completely changed my life. I'll be forever grateful to you."

NORA'S STORY

As a result of attending a Dressing Your Truth® training, Nora now feels a confidence and sureness about herself that had previously eluded her. She had been living as a Type 2 energy her entire adult life. Even in the workshop, after the Types were taught, and the participants were asked to divide themselves into the groups they thought they belonged to, Nora put herself into the Type 2 group. Later she learned that many women take on the energy that was prevalent in their upbringing.

The facilitator came around and immediately could see by Nora's physical characteristics that she was in the wrong group, and she asked Nora to step into the Type 4 group. Well, when she stepped into the Type 4 group, she magically felt a shift in her energy. It really happened that fast, in the blink of an eye. She was elated!

All her life she has been quiet and introverted, and took it as being shy. But in reality, Nora is not shy—she just is quiet by nature, which is a characteristic of the constant, still energy of the Type 4.

Learning her Type of beauty brought an understanding about many aspects of herself that are so validating. She says: "With the shift came a whopping ah-ha, as in, 'Now that's why I'm like that,' and 'Now this is the real me.'"

After the training, Nora was giddy for weeks! She integrated the information about Type 4s quickly and today, many months later, she is still grateful every day for what she learned. She feels stronger and more confident, and more importantly, kinder and more tolerant toward others.

SUMMARY OF THE TYPE 4 BOLD, STRIKING WOMAN

Carbon/earth is Type 4 energy. A Type 4 has a constant and exact energy. You are reflective and thorough, with an unerring eye for perfecting things. Your dominant shape in physical features is a straight line, visible in the parallel lines on the side of your face, straight hairline, and your typically erect posture.

As a Type 4 you may have a tendency toward these strengths:

- You move in a direct, straightforward line from Point A to Point B and you accomplish many tasks in this manner.

- You are poised and still with very little movement, and you have a regal countenance.

- You are clear and precise in your language and manner.

- You have a laser-like mental focus.

- You have a quietness and serenity about you that speaks volumes.

- You are stable and consistent. People trust you.

- You easily follow and obey rules, if you trust the source of those rules or if you feel that following them will lead you to a greater end.

- You have a keen eye that sees clearly what needs to be done to improve, perfect and streamline things and make it so others can reproduce it in a cost-effective manner.

- You are contemplative and seek more knowledge and wisdom.

- You are a pillar of strength and can anchor all those who surround you.

- You are captivating and mesmerizing and reflect to others an air of sophistication.

- You stay on track when you start something, and it's important to finish what you start.

As a Type 4, you may have a tendency toward these weaknesses:

- You may be cold and distant, content to live in your own world, building emotional walls around you so others do not approach you or know how to talk to you.

- You can be too authoritative, bossy or condescending.

- You may appear harsh, judgmental or too opinionated.

- You can get stuck in perfecting things, bringing your forward movement to a standstill.

TYPE 4 BEAUTY KEY WORDS

Alluring	Moderate
Astute	Modern
Black and white	Mysterious
Bold	Neat
Captivating	Noble
Chic	Notable
Classic	Opulent
Clean	Poised
Clear	Polished
Commanding	Precise
Concise	Professional
Conservative	Proper
Contemporary	Queenly
Contrasting	Refined
Cool	Reflective
Cultured	Regal
Defined	Scintillating
Designer look	Serene
Dignified	Serious
Diplomatic	Sleek
Discreet	Smooth
Distinctive	Sophisticated
Distinguished	Stark
Dramatic	Statuesque
Elite	Still
Enticing	Striking
Exact	Strong
Exotic	Stunning
Extravagant	Stylized
Extreme	Suave
Formal	Tailored
Impressive	Thorough
Independent	Tranquil
Lavish	Vivid
Look of wealth	Vogue
Majestic	Well-structured
Mesmerizing	Zealous

Part 4

- It's Time to Know What Type of Woman You Are

It's Time to Know what Type of Woman You Are

NOW THAT YOU HAVE READ THROUGH THE FOUR TYPES OF WOMEN, it is time for you to decide which Type is your dominant expression. Like I previously said, I believe you know in your heart who you truly are. However, we can be at odds with our true nature due to different life experiences that have caused us to feel ashamed, embarrassed and in judgment of ourselves. If you are uncertain of your Type or how to proceed, I offer you the following suggestions and support to help you come to terms with the true nature of who you are.

GUESSING OR AVOIDING YOUR TRUTH

Maybe you are trying to guess what Type of woman you are. That is just an avoidance technique, so go deeper and ask yourself what are you afraid of.

Are some uncomfortable feelings coming up?

Believe me, it is way more uncomfortable to live a lie than to finally, once and for all, own your true self and clear out all the lies and illusions you have been carrying around.

Let whatever feelings come up, come up! Only if you face those feelings can you overcome them. Unless you face them, they will hold you back and keep you hiding from yourself. Don't be afraid of who you really are. When you discover and accept the truth about yourself, it will set you free.

Isn't that what you really want?

Along the same lines as guessing, you could be putting off taking the next steps because you are avoiding taking full responsibility for your life.

Playing the victim is a popular way to experience life. When we think the power is outside of us and that we don't have a choice, it excuses us from action and we don't have to take responsibility for our lives.

If you are in this place, I highly recommend my best-selling book *Remembering Wholeness: A Personal Handbook for Thriving in the 21st Century*. It will guide you through a complete process to overcoming victim thinking once and for all.

Here are the most common tendencies that each Type of woman uses to keep herself stuck and in avoidance:

TYPE 1: Telling yourself stories and making excuses that convince you that you don't have the right or the power to choose something better for yourself. I have heard a lot of Type 1 women say things like, "I can't learn how to dress my truth because my husband wouldn't allow it," or, "Sorry, I just don't have the money."

TYPE 2: Telling yourself you need more information, more questions answered. Hesitant to take the next step, you procrastinate taking the steps necessary to move forward.

TYPE 3: Moving so swiftly through life and having your head buried in so many projects and to-do lists, you entirely miss feeling and experiencing your true nature and the true nature of others.

TYPE 4: Finding fault with the resources and support you have attracted into your life that are meant to help you move forward. Your gift of critiquing has turned into a pattern of criticizing.

YOUR RESPONSE TO THE DIFFERENT
STYLES OF EACH TYPE

You may think that a good way to know what Type of woman you are is to notice your response to the different styles of the four Types in the *Dressing Your Truth*® images you have seen. For example, you may be thinking, "Oh, I am a Type 4 because I love that style." Or, "I am a Type 2 because I love the softer styles." There are many instances where women have mislead themselves using this reference as an assessment tool.

The fashion world has taught us to look at an outfit and then to have an opinion on whether we like it or not, but has not considered if the outfit itself would actually look good on different types of women. In other words, the focus is on the outfit, not the women. Realistically, we can say that, yes, the outfit is beautiful, but we can't say it would look great on everyone!

You may be a Type 1 that is drawn to a Type 4 look because you are overly sensitive about coming across as silly if you dress true to your Type 1 nature. Or, you may be a Type 2 that is drawn to a Type 1 look, thinking you need to lighten up your appearance, that you would feel too drab in the Type 2 style. You may be a Type 3 that has attempted to soften your more dynamic nature for most of your life and so you think Type 2 clothes are best for you, therefore you are drawn to them. Or you may be a Type 3 that thinks I am a Type 4 since I look good in black! You may also be a Type 4 that is in conflict with your straightforward, bold nature that is drawn to a different Type's style in an effort to counter what you may deem a weakness in yourself.

> ARE YOU OVERWEIGHT AND DEPRESSED? THIS COULD BE A RESULT OF NOT LIVING TRUE TO YOUR NATURE.

Whatever the reason, using this approach as an assessment tool will most likely mislead you rather than help you know what Type of woman you are. Too many women have been trained to believe that they look good in certain styles because they want to look hip or trendy or fashionable, when actually that does not work so well when it comes to honoring their Type of beauty.

I am drawn to each of the four Types of beauty, and I love all the styles when they are on the right woman. Yes, I love them all! But I know that, as a Type 3, I am going to look my very best when I dress true to my Type 3 nature. You will be drawn to styles that match your true nature, but be aware that, if you have some unresolved feelings about your nature, you may be attracted to styles that aren't a good match for your inner beauty.

WHAT TYPE PUSHES YOUR EMOTIONAL BUTTONS?

Another clue to knowing what Type of woman you are is noticing which Type pushes your emotional buttons the most. You may have been so severely judged and shamed as a little girl, and you may have carried that shame and judgment into your adult life. These feelings lead to an aversion and disgust for who you are, but you are only aware of them through your judgment of other women of your Type.

Life is a mirror reflecting back to us how we deeply feel about ourselves. These deeper feelings of judgment have been hidden from you, and, after coming in contact with this material, you are now getting in touch with them.

You will not be the first woman to have acquired an illusionary hate for yourself!

In fact it is too common, but come on ladies, look at the statistics of women who are overweight and depressed. That could be a result of not living true to your nature. I used to be one of those statistics. I am convinced the chronic depression I have dealt with throughout my life was directly related to my inability to know myself and live my truth!

Before I end this section, I want to point out to you the two most common cop-outs women use these days to avoid living their truth and taking responsibility for their lives.

The most common pattern that women use to stay in avoidance is to use money as an excuse. "I don't have enough money" is an easy cop-out these days. Maybe it appears in your bank account that you don't have enough money. I believe, and have taught tens of thousands of women and men through my wealth mastery teachings, that when you passionately want something and it is right and timely for you, all you have to do is desire it and the money will come from wherever it is right now. (You can get support for clearing your patterns of lack and scarcity with money with the materials listed in the resource section at the back of this book.)

The second most common reason, and it could be a tie with the first, is "My husband!" Quite honestly, I am really tired of hearing women defaulting to their husbands and making them the reason they can't experience the fullness of who they are.

Why do you think husbands hold back? It is because of you! If you have an equal standing and partnership with your husband, as you should, why do you let him be the reason why you don't express your true self?

Some of the most common husband excuses are: "My husband will get upset if I spend the money!" "My husband doesn't want me to cut my hair!" "My husband doesn't believe in all this healing stuff." "My husband likes me the way I am."

"My husband is my excuse—I own it!—and he's an easy cop-out for me to use, because deep down I am scared of really knowing myself and living as big as I can as a woman!"

If it's not your husband who is playing this role for you, consider who else might be holding you back from experiencing you true nature. Is it your mother, a sister, a friend, a co-worker, or your hair stylist?

Ladies, stop hiding behind the husband or boyfriend or whatever excuse—step up, own your life and live it!

YOUR RESPONSE TO THIS BOOK

How you respond to the information in this book, and how you read this book says a lot about who you are. The following tendencies for each Type will be very accurate in classifying your response and reading of this book by Types:

TYPE 1: Because of your tendencies to not want to eliminate possibilities, you believe it is possible to be all four Types. A lot of Type 1s have this response, "I see all four types in me!" Because you have the most adaptable energy you are the chameleons of the Types and have an ability to adapt to the other three Types that are not dominant in you. You may have also not bothered to read the entire book, but bounced around through the sections and found one that sounded good and decided, "Oh, that's me!"

TYPE 2: Because you have a questioning nature, you will question yourself and second-guess yourself about who you are. You may even be skeptical about the *Dressing Your Truth®* system having legitimacy and accuracy. You will read and re-read the information over and over more than any other Type, and take a long time to come to a conclusion. You will be likely to ask a friend or associate what they think about the ideas in this book. You will seek a second opinion before drawing a conclusion yourself.

TYPE 3: It may have been hard for you to read from the front of the book to the back. You like to get to the point, fast, and pass by anything that appears to be too much detail. You may have even gone to the back of the book first, to see where this is going and what the end result is. You like to finish things quickly and get on to the next thing. You may have even read the book in this manner and are telling yourself, "Oh, I am Type 2!" which you are not because a Type 2 would never read this book that way!

TYPE 4: You may be thinking, "Carol Tuttle is full of it!" and "I am not going to Dress My Truth just because too many women are into this, and I don't want to be part of a fad!" I agree nobody knows you like you know yourself. You are the ultimate authority and your response may be getting in your way of allowing supportive information to come into your life, to help you live as boldly and fully and beautifully as you are designed to live.

HOW DO YOU MOVE THROUGH LIFE?

Another way to understand a lot about yourself and to discover who you truly are is by observing how you move through life. The little unedited movements of daily life will help you see your Type. How do you get your daily chores done? How do you move through the grocery store or the mall? How do you pack for a vacation?

TYPE 1: Unstructured and more carefree, finding delight in simple pleasures.

TYPE 2: Steadily and calmly enjoying what brings you and others comfort.

TYPE 3: Swiftly focusing on the end results with determination.

TYPE 4: Straight forwardly, concisely and precisely knowing where you stand with yourself and others.

WHAT ARE SOME OF YOUR MOST COMMON EXPRESSIONS AND PHRASES?

Another way to understand a lot about yourself and to discover who you truly are is by observing the things you say and what words you choose. Here are some of the most common phrases and words used by each Type:

TYPE 1: You might light-mindedly make fun of someone then quickly say, "Just kidding." When you like something, you say, "That is so fun!" It is common for you to giggle while you talk.

TYPE 2: Due to your sensitive nature, you may find yourself apologizing more than necessary. Before you ask a question, you will say, "I have a question."

TYPE 3: You can speak things abruptly and in a very direct manner. You say out loud (or at least in your mind) the following when you feel someone is taking too long to explain something, "Get to the point."

TYPE 4: When agreeing with others, your favorite exclamation is "Exactly!" You also use the word perfect frequently when you feel something has turned out to your liking.

YOUR CHILDHOOD

Look back to your childhood—way back! I mean when you were 2, 3, and 4 years old. What was your natural expression? What were you known for as a little girl? What were you praised for and even disciplined for? Here is a quick summary of some of the positive and negative things you may have been told as a little girl—the negatives quite possibly shut down your true nature:

TYPE 1: Stop moving. You're such a busy little girl. You are too hyper. You are too bouncy. You live in a dream world. Settle down. On the positive side: You are so much fun to be around. You make friends so easily. You dance and sing so well.

TYPE 2: You are shy. You are too sensitive. Hurry up, you take too long. You ask too many questions. You may have been the Type of little girl who was uncomfortable your first day of school, did not like sleepovers and hated it when you were left with a baby-sitter you did not know. On the positive side: You are so nice and kind. You are sweet. You are so easy-going and easy to get along with. How many collections did you say you have had?

TYPE 3: You are too demanding. You are too pushy. You are such a tomboy. You need to be more ladylike. You are too rough. Calm down, relax. On the positive side: You get things done so quickly. You're a natural leader. What a great athlete! You always know just what you want and go for it!

TYPE 4: You need to be more social. You are such a loner. You are such a quiet little girl. You need to make more friends and be more outgoing. You are so picky. You're such a know-it-all. You are too serious. You need to smile more. On the positive side: You act so grown up. Everybody knows where you stand on an issue. You are so independent. Your room is immaculate! You are so neat! You are very trustworthy.

Part 5

- TAKE THE NEXT STEP:
  LEARN HOW TO DRESS YOUR TRUTH

- DON'T WAIT UNTIL YOU LOSE WEIGHT!

- YOU'RE NEVER TOO OLD TO DRESS YOUR TRUTH

TAKE THE NEXT STEP:
LEARN HOW TO DRESS YOUR TRUTH

AT THIS POINT, you have become acquainted with each of the four Types. You know the difference between the:

- Type 1: The Bright, Animated Woman

- Type 2: The Subtle, Soft Woman

- Type 3: The Rich, Dynamic, Woman

- Type 4: The Bold, Striking Woman

You should have by now a clear idea of who you are from the inside out and what Type of woman you are. If you are like most woman, you don't accept this instantly. In fact, you may be in turbulent denial for a time. But slowly, the truth will win you over. The realization that innate qualities have been unacknowledged or suppressed often brings women to tears. But when you recognize the truth of who you are and accept it, it will bring you great joy and peace mind.

Sharing the truth of who you are in your appearance will change your life in a profound way. Every day of your life, you send a message to the world and to the people you interact with—a silent but powerful message of who you are. Every day that you put on clothes, makeup, jewelry and accessories that are hiding your true self, you are sending the opposite message of who you are to others.

Dressing Your Truth® is your next step in taking full ownership of your beauty and your truth. Having the tools to adorn yourself with the clothes, jewelry, accessories and makeup and the best color, cut and style for your hair that harmonize with your true inner nature, is an incredibly rewarding and deeply affirming experience for a woman. It is incredibly validating and freeing for women to finally have the skills and expertise necessary to take charge of their beauty, especially when most of us have grown up at odds with the way we think we look.

The most common practice women use in wardrobing themselves is to look at a fashionable outfit and then try to copy it. This practice does not hone your own beauty's sixth sense. *Dressing Your Truth*® teaches you a formula that speaks and honors your Type of beauty as a woman, so you have the skills to choose clothes and put together outfits, no matter what your level of dress or activity. Whether you're a stay at home mom that dresses casually, or a high-powered business woman that dresses professionally, you will have the skills you need for any level of dress. You will learn how to put together casual, athletic, professional, and even formal looks as well. As you have already heard me say, *Dressing Your Truth*® makes you your own beauty expert!

I invite you to take the important next step in living your truth fully as a woman, to learn the tools to dress your truth and then to take that information and create your own personal style that honors the Type of woman you are!

As I said in the first pages of this book, my team and I have created an interactive, online experience, including separate courses for each Type, to teach you how to dress your truth. Because of the visual, interactive nature of online learning and the advanced technology we have used, it turns out to be the best medium to teach *Dressing Your Truth*® to as many women in the world as possible.

It is important to remember that dressing true to your Dominant Type is the best choice to make. After years of research in developing *Dressing Your Truth®*, I know what will bring out your greatest beauty. If you are a Type 4, you learn how to dress like a Type 4 if you want to create a Type 4 appearance for yourself! That is how the program works! You dress true to you.

What you will learn in the online *Dressing Your Truth®* courses and experience is how to dress true to your nature by learning the five elements of *Dressing Your Truth®* for your Type. Those five elements that are a feature in every article of clothing you buy include:

- Design Lines

- Texture

- Fabrication

- Pattern

- Color/Chroma

In the three-hour *Dressing Your Truth®* course, which you will own for life, you will also be taught:

- What jewelry and accessories are best for you.

- What makeup is best and how to apply it to honor your facial features.

- What color, cut and style of hair is best for you, along with the proper terms to use when you go to your stylist so you speak their language and get what you want. We also have over 50 images per Type of short, medium and long hair styles that you can print and take to your stylist.

- If you have curly hair and you spend a lot of time straightening it, you are going to love the "How to do Curly Hair Perfectly" segment taught by my Type 2 daughter, Anne. In her 2-ness, she figured out the perfect steps and made a plan for how to get the most amazing curl from your hair. It is easy and simple to learn and you are going to love your curly hair and take a lot of your time back now that you no longer have to straighten it.

- Ongoing learning every month at our *Dressing Your Truth*® Club Nights that are broadcast live via the internet. At these monthly Club Nights, we continue to teach you how to bring out your personal style using *Dressing Your Truth*® with topics like: Ruffles for Every Type, How to Dress Your Professional Truth, How to Bring Your Secondary Energy in to Create Your Personal Style, Colors You Might Not Think You Can Wear.

- And much, much more!

I have been a pioneer in the self-help field for over 20 years. I have created a lot of resources through books and other media products. I have had the opportunity to find ways to use the technology of the Internet to deliver my work and teachings to help people all over the world. To date, I feel that *Dressing Your Truth*® is one of my best creations so far. What we have created with our interactive online courses has never been done before in the world of fashion and beauty. Have fun with it!

DON'T WAIT UNTIL YOU LOSE WEIGHT!

OKAY, LET'S TAKE ON THIS ISSUE, BECAUSE IT'S A BIG ONE FOR WOMEN! You may be thinking, "I will learn to dress my truth just as soon as I lose some weight!" Stop right there!

Waiting until you lose weight will only delay your body's ability to take the weight off naturally and effortlessly. "How is that possible?" you may be asking yourself. Let me explain this to you. In your current mind-set of thinking you have to lose weight first, you are creating a severe negative judgment towards your body. You are actually reinforcing the belief your body is not good enough. When you are in that judgment, it is actually harder for your body to shed the pounds.

I didn't quite expect to see what I have seen with our overweight, even obese *Dressing Your Truth®* clients. Once they started to dress their truth, they started to effortlessly lose weight. As I pondered on this, it began to totally make sense. It was happening for these primary reasons:

- They no longer were hating their bodies. In fact, they were beginning to feel good about themselves again, and to love themselves again. In my work as an energy healing therapist over the years, I learned first-hand that love was a more powerful influence than hate in allowing the body to heal.

- They changed their focus from being preoccupied with losing weight to now loving and adorning their body just the way it was. Whatever we focus on persists. And the simple act of these women changing their focus allowed their bodies to start releasing the weight with more ease.

Many women have gained weight due to the deeper belief that who they are is inadequate. The weight represents a form of hiding your true self from the world, an outer layer of protection created by your inner view of yourself. Also, when you are emotionally focused on the discomfort of being overweight, you may be distracting yourself from deeper feelings of inadequacy and hurt you are now ready to heal.

Michelle recently posted the following comment on my Facebook wall: "Every time I walked in to my closet I used to feel doom and gloom! I thought I didn't feel good in my clothes because I was not my ideal weight. I am still not my ideal weight, but since learning how to dress my truth I feel like I look good. I haven't felt that way for years. And all thanks to this remarkable new way of seeing myself."

ROCHELLE'S STORY

Rochelle wrote to me, sharing her story of how she believes Dressing Your Truth® helped her lose weight and reclaim her health back. She shares her life-changing story here.

"Dressing Your Truth® has impacted my life in a positive way. For the first time in many years, I look in the mirror and see someone who is attractive. My weight has been an issue for many years and has affected my health physically and mentally. I believe taking the Dressing Your Truth® online course has resulted in a 10 pound weight loss. I feel better about me and who I am. I want to sing the song from West Side Story, "I Feel Pretty." Feeling pretty is something I have not felt in many years.

"I used to weigh 300 pounds and was able to take off 70. I have struggled with taking off the rest of the weight for the last three years. Within a three week period I lost 10 pounds. When I am tempted to eat something that will keep the weight on, my mood changes to positive self talk as I tell myself, 'No, let's see what else I can eat to satisfy my hunger, and keep me healthy, happy and looking good.'

"Thank you for sharing Dressing Your Truth®. You are saving my life emotionally and physically. I am excited to get dressed each day and my emotional life is improving. I am looking forward to each new day in a positive manner expecting the best."

Start loving your body exactly where it is right now by learning to Dress Your Truth. Your body will thank you by letting go of the unwanted weight it does not want to carry around for you anymore and naturally respond to your new focus of loving yourself just the way you are!

You're Never Too Old to Dress Your Truth

If you think you are too old to Dress Your Truth, just stop it! You are never too old to improve yourself and to develop the woman that you are. We have worked with clients from as young as 9 to as old as 82. Are you ever too old to look gorgeous? No!

Alice comes to mind, a tender, loving woman of 82 who came to learn *Dressing Your Truth*® at our center in Utah. She was so excited to discover her true nature and expressed to us at the training, "I am so glad to know who I am before I die! And to start showing to the world how beautiful I am."

So, if your belief is "I am too old to dress my truth," it is going to be a short conversation. All I have to say is "Don't deny yourself. Get going. It's time to take some action, to start dressing your truth now!"

Part 6

The Biggest Fashion Myths

I WANT TO HELP YOU LET GO OF SOME OF THE BIGGEST FASHION MYTHS that have been confusing women for decades. I mean, who made up these rules anyway?

Fashion Myth #1: Black, Black, Black— What's with All the Black?

AT A RECENT DRESSING YOUR TRUTH® EVENT a woman with a dominant Type 3 Energy came up to me and said, "I wore black just because you said I shouldn't!"

I responded, "How Type 3 of you to do that! You can wear whatever you want!" I then shared with the audience, "For most of you, if you want to look 10 years older, 10 pounds heavier, and feel crummy, just keep wearing black!"

I have helped thousands of women learn to dress their truth. Repeatedly, I experience women nearly "freaking out" when they learn they have to give up their black clothes if they are going to dress their truth.

This is amazing to me. You would think I was telling them they can't wear yellow, or blue, or maybe even a very beautiful version of purple! It's BLACK I'm talking about, ladies, no movement, no expression, just stillness, and on most women, it's deadly.

All I can figure is the fashion gods got together years ago and said, "Let's fool the women of the world and convince them that the color everyone should wear is the color that will look the worst on most of them!" And everybody was convinced! The clothing merchandisers would want everyone to keep wearing black so they can keep pumping out black clothes really cheap and keep you buying them.

Let's look at black through a vibrational/movement lens. Imagine a scale where one end of the scale represents no movement and the other end of the scale represents very high movement. Where would you place black on that scale? Black is exact and still. Black would go on the no-movement side of the scale.

As you have learned three of the 4 Types of beauty have a very different movement in their personality, body language and physical features than the movement of exact and still! When you put black on a Type 1, 2, or 3 woman, it is in conflict with her true movement and natural beauty.

Here are some of the most famous misconceptions about black that are not true:

- **BLACK MAKES YOU LOOK THINNER.** Not at all, it actually inflates you and makes you look bigger since the color black is so still.

- **EVERYONE LOOKS GOOD IN BLACK.** Wrong! Only women with a dominant Type 4 energy look stunning in black. Type 1s look childish, Type 2s look overpowered, and Type 3s just look plain old. And if you are not a Type 4, the darkness of black will pick up in your face, accentuating the lines and movement of your face that will then look like imperfections and flaws in your skin.

- **BLACK FRAMES YOUR SILHOUETTE.** Well, if that is the case, I don't want it on my body! It would only make me look bigger than I really am. Black is a saturated, bold color and will look heavy on anyone who is not a bold woman.

- **BLACK IS THE COLOR THAT GOES WITH EVERYTHING**. You have been convinced the color black is a neutral color. It is not. It really only looks great with other saturated colors or pure stark white—on a Type 4!

- **I WON'T KNOW WHAT TO WEAR IF I CAN'T WEAR MY BLACK.** Please let me help you figure that one out (see "Substitutes for Black for Each Type of Woman" later in this section). I guarantee you will be thanking me and in the near future be saying to me, "I can't imagine wearing black again." I have heard that countless times.

What do you believe about wearing black? Are you convinced you can't give it up?

Join the thousands of women worldwide who are getting rid of their black and bringing vitality and true beauty back to their lives!

Here are the reasons each Type is drawn to black.

TYPE 1: A Type 1 may feel a need to be taken more seriously, but she winds up looking silly because the contrast is so severe. When a Type 1 dresses her truth—leaving black out of her wardrobe—the atmosphere around her is lightened, she is better understood and more readily accepted for who she is.

TYPE 2: The color is so widely accepted and everyone says it works, so a Type 2 doesn't question it as she might otherwise. Black on a Type 2 will make her look washed out and faded away. If she learns to dress her truth (without the black) she will stand out in subtle confidence.

TYPE 3: A Type 3 might think that black is a power color and she will be attracted to that, but it will look harsh on her. She will look older, more textured and overweight. However, her *Dressing Your Truth®*

179

look—without black—will give her a confident, sure, dynamic and exotic look.

TYPE 4: A Type 4 can actually wear black! However, she will sometimes grow tired of it and be looking for more variety. *Dressing Your Truth®* will show you how to add variety without all the frumpiness.

In conclusion, if you think you look good in black, but you are not a Type 4, you are settling for mediocrity. Let *Dressing Your Truth®* help you see and feel the difference. You will love it!

SUBSTITUTES FOR BLACK FOR EACH TYPE OF WOMAN

I understand it can seem stressful to let go of your black clothes, especially if you have a lot of them. I don't think it's because you particularly love and adore your black clothes. It most likely is because it seemed like an easy solution to the problem of not knowing what to buy in your effort to look your best. In a world of fashion that gives you very little guidance, we all had hoped that black was the answer to not knowing what color to buy.

Now are you hanging in a state of "If I have to give up my black, I am not sure I can get into this *Dressing Your Truth®* thing—it seems overwhelming!"? No worries. I am going to give you a great alternate color that is just one of your black replacements in the *Dressing Your Truth®* world. I show you these and several other choices in our *Dressing Your Truth®* online courses, where it is extremely helpful to see the visual examples of these alternatives.

TYPE 1: Dark chocolate brown is a great substitute for black for your bright/animated nature. Think of a dark chocolate candy bar, and you've got the right brown for you. It will look fresh, crisp and alive on you.

TYPE 2: Soft, muted brown is a great substitute for black for your subtle/soft nature. Think of a milk chocolate candy bar, and that is your color of brown. It will look elegant and comfortable on you.

TYPE 3: Rich golden brown is a great substitute for black for you. Think of a rich, golden dirt and that is the brown for you. It will look dynamic and substantial on you.

TYPE 4: Good news for you, black is a signature color for you because it is so still and exact. But I still have a tip for you! Make sure it is a very deep, saturated black, with no fading and no washing out. If the black is softened, it will look frumpy on you. The right black will look clean, simple and stunning on you.

FASHION MYTH #2:
EVERY WOMAN LOOKS GOOD IN WHITE!

OKAY, WE SUCCESSFULLY DEBUNKED the "black looks good on any woman" misconception. Now let's go after the color white.

White is a staple in most women's wardrobes. But believe it or not, it does not work for everyone. In fact, stark white does not work for most women!

As you have been learning, every woman has a unique natural movement that is expressed in her body language, physical features, and overall approach to life—her Type. We look our best when we wear colors that match our natural movement and expression.

Just as we did with black, let's look at white through a vibrational/movement lens. Imagine a scale where one end of the scale represents no movement and the other end of the scale represents very high movement. Where would you place stark white on that scale? White is still, constant, plain and pure. White is color with nothing added. Just like black, it would go on the no-movement side of the scale.

If you are the Type of woman with a buoyant or higher, more dynamic nature (Type 1 and Type 3), white is going to appear as though it is sitting on top of your body rather than becoming a part of your whole expression of beauty. Although Type 1s can get away with wearing pure white if they have other colors that are true to their Type with it, there are some better choices for you. If you are a woman with a more subdued nature (Type 2), white is way too stark and cold for your natural warmth and comforting style. Women with a more structured, stylized nature (Type 4) look best in stark white.

SUBSTITUTES FOR WHITE FOR EACH TYPE OF WOMAN

Here is another *Dressing Your Truth®* tip for each Type of woman, a great alternate color that is just one of your white replacements. I show you these and several other color choices in our *Dressing Your Truth®* online courses, where it is extremely helpful to see the visual examples of these alternates.

TYPE 1: Because your natural movement is more buoyant and spontaneous, you will look best in winter white. Your naturally sunny nature is honored by the warmth of winter white.

TYPE 2: Your natural movement is more subdued and gentle, so you will look best in eggshell white. Adding this grayed undertone supports your relaxed, calm approach to life.

TYPE 3: Because your natural movement is more swift and dynamic, you will look best in a shade of light tan that we call wheat. This golden tan color honors your rich and substantial approach to life.

TYPE 4: Your natural movement is more exact and constant, and you look great in white. You will look best in a pure, clean stark white. Make sure it is the whitest of white as this honors your simple, precise approach to life.

Note: Don't throw out your white clothes yet! After you take the *Dressing Your Truth®* course, you will know how to dye your whites to be the correct color for your Type.

Knowing your true nature and natural movement—matching your clothing to honor your natural expression—will bring out your true beauty to a level that will even surprise yourself so giving up your white will not be a sacrifice. Believe me, if you are a Type 1, 2, or 3, you won't miss it!

FASHION MYTH #3:
COCO CHANEL AND THE LITTLE BLACK DRESS

COCO CHANEL WAS A PIONEERING FRENCH DESIGNER whose modernist philosophy made her an important influence in the early 20th century. She had an extraordinary influence on fashion in the beginning years of the fashion industry which dramatically set the industry into motion in the 1920s.

> BEFORE COCO, WOMEN WERE STILL LIVING IN THE DISCOMFORT OF CORSETS AND HEAVY, LONG DRESSES

She did a lot of good with her ideas and insights that helped women to dress more simply and to diversify the fashion world. Before Coco, women were still living in the discomfort of corsets, heavy, long dresses with long sleeves, and a lot of lace.

True to her Type 4 nature (do a Google search for Coco Chanel and click on Images—her face screams Type 4!), she took on the fashion world in a bold way and made it better. In fact, some might even say she created the fashion world!

Along with the value she contributed, true again to her Type 4 nature, she created some fashion rules that are still operating, rules that are so incredibly misleading and outdated it makes me laugh! I am sure Coco could not help this—being a Type 4, she felt she knew better than anyone what was right for every woman!

One of the most outdated, cliché fashion rules that I am very excited to blow out of the water is the "little black dress" theory which came from Coco. "The 'little black dress' is considered essential to a complete wardrobe by many women who believe it a basic rule that every woman should own a simple, elegant black dress that can be dressed up or down depending on the occasion: for example, worn with a jacket and pumps for daytime business wear or with more ornate jewelry and accessories for evening. A wardrobe staple for a number of years, the style of the little black dress ideally should be as simple as possible: a short black dress that is too clearly part of a trend would not qualify because it would soon appear dated." (From Wikipedia.)

Really, let's look at this from a Type 3, practical point of view! If you are not a little woman, you are not going to look good in a little black dress. And, if you are not a Type 4, the simple, classic design line of the little black dress is not the right movement for you! If I were to wear a little black dress I would look like a very large, old lady. The color black is death to most women's natural beauty!

Thanks Coco for what you did for women's fashion, but it is time to throw out the "little black dress" rule and the "every woman can wear black rule!" Read on and discover the other misconceptions you have bought into and continue to take back your true beauty!

Fashion Myth #4: There is One Type of Beauty—The Type 4 World of Beauty!

IF YOU WERE TO PICK UP A CURRENT ISSUE OF VOGUE magazine, you would find that nearly every woman featured in the magazine's articles, editorials, pictorials and advertisements in the magazine is a Type 4 woman.

The physical features of very tall Type 4 women depict a beauty of perfect symmetry and balance in their physical features. If any of the models lead with any other Type they have a very strong secondary Type 4 in their profile that is strongly expressed in their physical features.

To illustrate, the following are all considered to be supermodels who are either Type 4s or who have a strong secondary Type 4: Twiggy (Type 4), Christie Brinkley (Type 1 with strong secondary Type 4), Kate Moss (Type 4), Claudia Schiffer (Type 4), Naomi Campbell (Type 4), Heidi Klum (Type 4), Gisele Bündchen, (Type 3 with strong secondary Type 4), Cindy Crawford, (Type 3 with strong secondary Type 4), and Elle Macpherson (Type 4).

This Type 4 style typifies a beauty that we could call sleek and stunning, with porcelain skin, perfectly set features, refined and statuesque. I agree that Type 4 women and their natural features are incredibly beautiful—it's the kind of reflective beauty we have a hard time taking our eyes off of!

Hands down, every skin care model that is pitching us skin care products is a Type 4 woman. What this means is she naturally has very smooth skin with very fine, small pores that naturally gives her porcelain skin a sleek and youthful look. She does not even need the product she is attempting to sell us. It is not the product that she is selling that is making her skin this way, it is her Type 4 skin that is a part of her natural beauty.

As a Type 3 with Type 3 skin, I can never make my more textured, deeper facial lines, and pigmented skin look like Type 4 skin with any product. I could believe that my skin could not be as beautiful as Type 4 skin. The fashion and beauty world certainly led me to believe that. And if I believed that, I would either hate my appearance or would be investing heavily in products and methods to alter my unique beauty as so many women do.

Unfortunately, this standard of beauty leaves little room for other Types of beauty, at least not in the fashion world. This has created a standard of beauty that ignores and overlooks the naturally beauty of the other three Types of women. I have witnessed an equal and compelling beauty in Type 1, Type 2, and Type 3 women when given the tools to honor and dress their beauty with *Dressing Your Truth*®.

Nevertheless, some beauty companies are willing to do it differently. I applaud Cover Girl, the American cosmetics company, for featuring Type 1 women as the face of their brand. In the 1960s, Cybil Shepherd, a Type 1, was the Cover Girl model offering us a fresh, wholesome look. In the 1970s, Christie Brinkley followed in her footsteps. The current face of Cover Girl is Ellen Degeneres, another Type 1, which pretty much breaks all standards of the fashion and beauty industry—a 51-year-old woman who is only 5' 7" tall and did not make her fame in the fashion and beauty world. There is also Drew Barrymore (Type 1) who has appeared numerous times for Cover Girl products. Kudos to Cover Girl for offering us the image of a different Type of beauty.

FASHION MYTH #5: YOU LOSE YOUR BEAUTY WHEN YOU AGE!

IN MY RESEARCH, I HAVE DISCOVERED that the younger you are the more you can pull off trends and styles and still look pretty good. But, the older you get, the more having the wrong hairstyle and wearing what is not right for your Type of beauty ages you—fast!

When you are wearing a hair color and style that is in conflict with your Type of beauty, the more accentuated are the features you have deemed as flaws. Every Type of woman can have long, medium, and short hairstyles: it's when the color, cut and style is not right for her Type—at any hair length—that it becomes an aging factor. Look at these examples of how the wrong hairstyle can age women ages 35 and up:

- If a Type 1 woman has let her hair grow below her shoulder blades and has a lot of ash highlights, it will pull her energy downward, which pulls her face down, thus aging her, and adding weight to her jaw line.

- If a Type 2 woman is sporting a bob haircut with gold high-lights, which puts her hairline right at her jaw, it will make her face look fat due to accentuating her fuller, blended cheek and jaw line.

- A Type 3 woman, for instance, who is wearing a saturated dark hair color parted down the middle, and that flows down below her chin with no layers, accentuates her deeper facial lines and more substantial nose, thus making her appear a good 10 to15 years older than she really is.

- If a Type 4 woman is wearing her hair in a soft, flowing style, it will make her appear old and frumpy as it conflicts with her more structured bone structure, making her appear more manly.

If you add clothing and jewelry that is in conflict with a woman's Type of beauty, you are adding the appearance of pounds and years to her.

Add this all up and you have created a huge need for the current trend in anti-aging products and methods. The anti-aging market has carved a billion dollar niche in the fashion and beauty industry, all because women have not been given the tools to honor their personal Type of beauty and bring it out! I feel confident in saying that the more women who learn to dress their truth, the more we will affect a decline in the need for anti-aging products and methods.

I love the example of confidence that Marsha (a Type 3) sets for all us when it comes to the fear of aging and losing our youthful looks. She recently posted the following on my Facebook wall:

"I'm 47 and, in the past, I've been terrified of getting old and looking old. I had an interesting moment a couple of days ago.... I realized that since starting to dress my truth in the last two months, I had had no fearful thoughts regarding getting or looking old. I feel like I can be my most beautiful self for the rest of my life. That is huge for me. It's like, 'Hey, bring it on, baby, 'cause I'm ready!'

Would there even be such a thing as a cosmetic surgery craze if every woman had the confidence Marsha displays? Read on.

I recently read an article in a fashion magazine that reported that 10.2 million people had cosmetic or non-surgical procedures in the United States in 2008. Four of the top five procedures preformed were: Botox injections, breast augmentation, rhinoplasty, and abdominoplasty. Or, in plain, everyday language, we're talking about wrinkle shots, boob jobs, nose jobs, and tummy tucks! Ironically, this report didn't have a tone of alarm but was more like a "join the party" invitation! This anti-aging craze surely attracts the baby boomer generation, and as a result, eternal youth has become a billion dollar industry.

I think it is safe to say that most of these 10.2 million people were women afraid of looking old before their time. It used to be that only the aging starlets of the world, the rich and famous, were using these procedures to secure eternal youth. Nowadays everyone in the neighborhood is doing it (or at least considering it as an option) and putting it on their credit cards.

What if there was a safe, natural way to take years off your appearance and pounds off your body, that did not involve invasive surgery, drugs, and MLM companies? Would you be interested?

The best anti-aging intervention I know of is the anti-aging hairstyle! What you are doing with the color, cut and style of your hair is the most influential aging or anti-aging influence in your life. Your hair frames your face and if you've got the wrong hairdo, I don't care how much plastic surgery you have, you just aren't going to look your best.

I have a gift for helping women choose the perfect color, cut and style for their face shape and bone structure that naturally takes years off their appearance. I have worked with thousands of women from all over the world who have come to me to discover what is right for them. I have many before and after pictures of these women and the pictures alone prove my point, some of which appear in the color section of this book. When you have the wrong color, cut and style of hair it is going to:

- Make your nose appear bigger

- Make your wrinkles appear deeper

- Make your chin appear fuller

- Make your teeth appear duller

- Make your eyes appear saggy

I would have loved to have had five minutes with those 10.2 million people seeking whatever-plasty to show them how naturally they could successfully achieve what their cosmetic procedures only attempted to do unnaturally.

I have seen it too many times to doubt it. Give yourself the best anti-aging formula I know of by getting the perfect color, cut and style to honor your natural features. What can this anti-aging hairstyle do for you? It will make your face look stunning.

- Make your nose appear more balanced

- Make your wrinkles fade away, disappear

- Make your chin tighten up, becomes more well blended

- Make your teeth appear whiter

- Make your eyes appear brighter

FASHION MYTH #6: MY HAIR STYLIST KNOWS BEST

HAIR IS A HUGE PART OF A WOMAN'S LOOK. Not having the right color, cut and style that harmonizes with your true nature can add unwanted years and even pounds to your face. When you learn to Dress Your Truth, you can honestly avoid having another bad hair day, ever.

A popular myth that is taught in the fashion world is to go with the opposite movement and shape of your face in a hairstyle to compliment and balance your face. For example a Type 3 jaw line is very angular. This myth would suggest that you choose a soft, flowing hairstyle to balance the more angular jaw line. This will not work, as it only accentuates the angles and makes a woman's jaw look larger and protruding. For a Type 1, who has a rounder face, this philosophy would suggest a longer, straighter hairstyle, to draw the face down, but this will accentuate the roundness, and the hair and face will be out of sorts. As is true for any Type of woman, Type 1s can have long hair—but straight, long hair with no layers will not be a Type 1's best look. It is best to choose a hairstyle that honors and compliments your face's natural movement, according to your Type of beauty. And it can be any length of hair.

Along with being misled by this hair fashion myth, here are the most common mistakes that women make that contribute to too many bad hair days:

193

USING THE WRONG COLOR ON YOUR HAIR. When you color your hair, you don't want it to look like you've colored it. When you color and highlight your hair, you want it to look completely natural and beautiful. If you choose the wrong color for you or your Type, it will stand out. For example, if a Type 2, subtle, soft woman is putting bright, golden highlights in her hair, it will drown out her face. When a woman's hair color is not right, you notice the hair color and not the woman.

STRAIGHTENING CURLY HAIR. I can always pick out a woman who is straightening her curly hair. It looks like straight hair with an underlying frizziness that is trying to peek through. Your hair's natural movement is the best look for you. If you have curly hair, that will look best on you. If you have straight hair, that is best for you. It shouldn't take you more than 10 to 20 minutes to do your hair and look fabulous. If it takes longer than that, you are not working with the natural movement of your hair. Trust the natural movement of your hair to be your best look.

NOT USING THE RIGHT HAIR PRODUCTS OR ANY PRODUCTS AT ALL. In the hair product world, you have probably noticed that there is a lot more than just shampoo and conditioner! There are pre-styling and finishing products that make all the difference in having a great hairstyle that honors the beauty in your face. Knowing the right product for the right style and the proper use of it makes all the difference.

> IT SHOULDN'T TAKE YOU MORE THAN 10 TO 20 MINUTES TO DO YOUR HAIR AND LOOK FABULOUS.

USING THE WRONG STYLING TOOLS. For example, when you should be using a flat iron, you may be using a curling iron, making your hair really bouncy when you would look better with an edgy style. Using the wrong size and kind of brushes, or not knowing how to use a flat iron to get your best look, are just a few of the tools to avoid problems that can prevent you from achieving your best look.

WAITING TOO LONG BETWEEN HAIR APPOINTMENTS. To keep up your best look and have fabulous hair, you need to get yourself to the salon on a regular basis. To keep up my short style and keep my gray hair colored, I go to the salon every four weeks. I am a firm believer that when you look great and feel great, life in every way shows up to support you. Whether it's manifesting more money or creating great health, investing in yourself is the number one key to creating every aspect of a fantastic life. I encourage you to get into the salon and keep your style up so that you really do feel good about yourself.

GIVING TOO MUCH POWER TO YOUR STYLIST. Before I had opened our *Dressing Your Truth*® Hair Salon, I was guilty of this, as most women are. What happens to our self-confidence and right to speak up when we sit in the stylist's chair? Wow, it's pretty crazy how we become mute and speechless about what we want and when we don't like what the stylist is doing. Deciding to change stylists when we are not satisfied with our hair can be like getting a divorce! Speak up ladies, you should be your own hair expert. There is a good chance that the hairstyle your stylist is suggesting for you has more to do with the Type of woman he or she is than the Type of woman you are!

The *Dressing Your Truth*® online course and experience teaches you exactly what you need to know to avoid these mistakes. You learn the perfect color, cut and style for you. You learn which products are best for you. We'll show you step by step instructions on how to use the products with the right tools. We take you from the towel on your head to your finished look. We also offer an excellent *Dressing Your Truth*® hair care line that gives you the selection of products you need to create a lot of great hair days.

Fashion Myth #7: You Have to Spend Lots of Money to Be Beautiful

AS A RESULT OF NOT KNOWING WHAT LOOKS BEST ON US, and thus not knowing what to buy, we waste an overwhelming amount of money on clothes, jewelry, accessories and makeup that we really don't love.

If you are like most women, you go into your closet, look at a rack full of clothes, and have to admit that there is very little in there that you can honestly say you love. Women often say that they do not love anywhere from 60 to 80 percent of their current wardrobe. That is why you stand in front of your closet and say, "I have nothing to wear!" Then your husband looks at you wondering why you can say such a thing when you have a closet chock full of clothes, shoes, handbags and accessories!

Most women have a limited budget when it comes to creating a great wardrobe. You may believe that it takes a lot of money to create one. You can't create a great wardrobe no matter how much money you have when you don't know how to buy what is right for you! As a result, you end up with a closet full of items you don't love and end up wasting your money time and time again. You had good intentions when you bought them, but if you are honest with yourself, you have to admit you don't love them.

In a recent survey we conducted, we discovered the following tendencies were common for women, that the average women has between $7,000 and $10,000 worth of clothing, shoes and other items in her closet. That is based on the average outfit (including a top, bottom, shoes, hose and a piece of jewelry) costing $175 to $225. If you consider that on average you don't like 60 percent of what is in your closet, you have about $4,000 to $6,000 worth of items that you have wasted money on!

Many of you acquire your wardrobes in $40 to $80 increments. This pattern is driven by the dilemma of not knowing what to buy and what looks best on you. As a result of your not feeling great about what you have purchased, you keep wearing the same old-same old day after day, feeling safe in a conservative wardrobe that is boring and uninspiring to you. You also have likely made purchases that are wrong for you, but which you don't feel you can return or wear. This makes you feel guilty and stuck.

There are many reasons why we end up with a closet full of clothes of different colors and styles that we don't love. It is common for you to choose clothes to hide as much of your body as possible, or at least any body parts you feel embarrassed or ashamed of. You may have been told that you have a big butt, arms, stomach or ankles. You feel very self-conscious about drawing attention to this part of your body, and attempt to cover it, hoping no one will notice this part of you. This may be your biggest incentive to purchase more and more clothes, once again wasting money on items that are not the best for your Type of beauty. It is quite possible that what you think is concealing your body is actually drawing more attention to what you don't want others to notice.

Another reason why your closet seems full of things you don't like is because you may feel like an item looked good at the store—and because the saleswoman influenced you—and then you get home and realize you don't like it. There is a lot of confusion over so many different trends you could be following, maybe you bought an outfit one day because you wanted to try out a trend, then you got home and decided that it wasn't for you.

You may be wasting money on clothes you don't love because you believe you have to conform to the standards you see around you. Because a job, a mother, a spouse, where you live or your culture often dictates what you wear, you may have taken on the idea that you have to squelch your own style and sense of beauty and conform to an outdated or uncomfortable standard. You fear you won't be accepted unless you conform to that obsolete standard, and you are afraid if you change your appearance, you may cause conflict with those close to you.

Looking professional is a good example of what many women conform to. Most women think a professional look is one consisting of a dark business suit with a white blouse and with little or no jewelry. When dressing your truth, you learn how much fun and variety you can bring to your professional style and even come across as more confident and professional than in your previous conservative look.

We recently did a survey of our *Dressing Your Truth*® clients in which we had 185 women respond. One of the questions we asked them was "Now that you are dressing your truth, how much of what is in your closet do you love and feel great in?" We had an overwhelmingly positive response! Over 90 percent of the women could honestly say that they loved 90 to 100 percent on what they owned.

These are just a few of the comments women shared with us in the survey: "Now everything goes together. I don't need separate shoes for this outfit and a bag for that one. I love it! And I look at my closet now and love everything in it." (Karen, Type 1.) "Prior to *Dressing Your Truth*®, I had about 60 percent of my clothing that I didn't wear. I love clothing so I had lots of stuff, but nothing I loved. Since I learned how to dress my truth, I love and wear everything in my closet now and spend a lot less money on clothing than I used to." (Susie, Type 3.)

Our goal is for you to love and wear every article of clothing in your closet, to have zero frustration when shopping, and for every part of you to look good and feel good in everything you have to wear—all this while spending far less money than you have spent in the past.

Fashion Myth #8: You Have to Be Skinny to Be Beautiful!

THIS BELIEF IS THE NUMBER ONE BODY IMAGE ISSUE that women unknowingly acquire at a very early age, and it continues to defeat us through most of our lives. As women, we take this belief on very early in our teen years, probably between ages 10 and 13, because as young girls we look outside of ourselves to consider what the world considers beautiful. With a fashion system that constantly shows us very thin, skinny women as the epitome of beauty, we default to believing skinny is more beautiful than not skinny. We unknowingly move in to our adult years with this limiting belief intact, always present to berate us and our bodies with it.

As I have mentioned elsewhere in this book, in a fashion world that shows skinny women as the model for beauty and also shows us mannequins that are a size 6, it is easy to believe "I have to be skinny to be beautiful."

When we go shopping and go into the dressing room to try on fashionable looking clothes (and which most likely are not right for your Type), and the clothes don't feel good or look good on you, you immediately conclude that the reason they don't look good is because you are too fat! You probably do a real number on yourself then, looking into the mirror and telling yourself, "I am too fat," and then continuing to shame specific parts of your body that you blame for not being attractive or thin enough.

You may have never considered that the real reason you don't feel good or look good in those clothes has more to do with the fact that they are not the right design lines, patterns, colors, etc. for your Type of beauty, and that their fit and feel have a lot less to do with the size of your body that with not matching your Type.

As I close this section on the biggest fashion myths, I invite you to take this myth and all the others I have noted and throw them out. It may take you a little longer to get rid of the "every woman can wear black" myth, but please release yourself from the "I have to be skinny to be beautiful" myth once and for all. This is the most damaging of the myths to your psyche and self-esteem.

Stop shaming your body and the size of it. Start loving yourself exactly as you are now! Start with this: commit to no longer saying "I am too fat!" I don't even care if you are overweight. What you tell your body, your body believes. Your beauty is not in the size of your body. Your beauty starts within you and continues as an outer expression of you! As you start to dress your truth and start loving your body, as a result, your body starts to get healthier and fitter due to the fact that you are now loving yourself just the way you are. Many women have told me that they have lost weight just by joyfully accepting and embracing their Type. It is just one of the miraculous results of changing your outlook on yourself and your beauty.

Part 7

- Loving Your New Look

- Shopping Your Truth—10 Great Rules

- Pay It Forward

- A Message To Teen Girls

- Top Celebs Dressing Their Truth

- My Parting Thoughts

Loving Your New Look

WHEN YOU TAKE THE DRESSING YOUR TRUTH COURSE, there may be some things that are new to you or you may even think "I would never wear that!" Believe me, I have heard it hundreds of times, yes, hundreds. Too many women are not living their truth and when they put truth on their body it can feel very different.

When you learn to Dress Your Truth, don't compare it with what you have been doing. *Dressing Your Truth*® is revolutionary and there is no other system like it out there.

When you fully understand the *Dressing Your Truth*® system, you won't ever be saying things like: "I hate silver jewelry!" or "I will never look good in that." Instead, you will be saying: "I know what jewelry is exactly right for me!" and "I always look good in that color." And, "Shopping is always so much fun. I can't wait to go!"

I encourage you to try our 30-day transformation. Once you have gone through the course (and you can get that in just a few hours!), commit to Dress Your Truth for the next 30 days.

I am a Type 3 and it is my nature to push you to dive right in and do it full on. You will never know the difference if you are still holding back or holding a lie on your body.

During those 30 days, you'll experience more confidence, happiness and freedom than ever before. And we're here to support you through every step of the way.

This new world of *Dressing Your Truth®* will soon make so much sense to you that when you begin to shop for new pieces, whether at a consignment shop, second hand thrift shop (which we love and recommend!) or name brand stores—it gets really easy to shop.

You will soon discover that the reason that the clothes you thought you liked don't flatter you, don't feel good on you, or actually make you appear heavier, is not because your body has a problem: it is the truth about what clothes look good on you!

Dressing Your Truth® reveals it's not about body type, it's not your age or race—it's about truth.

Many of our clients report they have lost weight when dressing their truth because it's no longer a struggle to hold a lie on their body.

As you move forward, you'll see that you aren't as preoccupied with how you feel, you won't be as self-conscious about your body and you definitely will be turning a few heads your way. Rightfully so! God created you to be beautiful!

You are designed to be beautiful—so be that way. If someone wonders what you are doing or why you have changed your appearance, just encourage them by saying, "I have made a decision to be true to myself and it feels great!" There's no reason to explain, to justify or to get into long discussions. Just be yourself, be happy and be confident—live your truth, fully you!

CAMILLE'S STORY

Camille's story teaches us a good lesson: when we own our lives and stop making excuses and take charge of who we are, others align and support us more fully in living our truth.

Camille attended a Dressing Your Truth® course in 2007. She thought it was wonderful. But when she got home, her husband was not the supportive, excited fan she had hoped for. It was hard for her to dress and do her makeup and hair due to the incredible resistance she felt from him.

She thought about it every day (how can you not think about it when you get dressed every day?). After about 10 months, she tried not to think about the Dressing Your Truth® program. She told herself that it just didn't matter.

Nevertheless, try as she may, she still thought about it every day! Another year went by, and Camille and her husband were constantly fighting about her weight, how she looked, or didn't look. It was crazy and frustrating.

Finally, one day she woke up and realized that if she were to live her truth, she needed to take better care of herself. She realized that the extra weight she was carrying was holding her back in her relationship with her husband and keeping her from pursuing her personal goals and dreams.

Camille started exercising consistently and eating nutritious foods in proper amounts. She went back to her closet and put together outfits that were true to her Type.

"Recently," she reports, "I purchased your online course for my Type. It was a fantastic refresher course. I also learned how to fix my Type 3 curly hair. This is the first time in many, many years that I love my hair. I now have a smile on my face when I get dressed. I love how I look. And guess what? My husband is dating me again!"

ONE LAST PERSONAL STORY

The following story will ring true to many women. It was given anonymously by a Type 2 woman.

"I am 34 years old, and I live in a small ski town in Idaho. Most people who live here dress in outdoor clothing, which can sometimes be drab and shapeless. I have lived here for 10 years and have

gone through a few wardrobe changes, mostly from one outdoor clothing company to the next.

"I have to say that the latest change with Dressing Your Truth® has been the most fun by far! I am constantly getting compliments about how well put together I look, which is so new for me and quite a change from my past. Now when I go out, I stand out from the jeans and fleeces everyone else is wearing. I get noticed, which is so fun for me as a Type 2 because I often feel blended into the background.

In my late teens, I decided that I had no idea how to dress fashionably, and so I began to dress like a boy. I wore baggy boy's shirts and jeans and felt a new kind of freedom that I wore what was comfortable and felt good in, and I didn't care about the fashion trends anymore. This philosophy carried into most of my 20s. I desired to look pretty and sexy, but I thought it just wasn't one of my talents to know what to wear.

"Then I turned 30. I wanted freedom from the boring clothes I had been wearing! I started to experiment with skirts and dresses and color, but quickly found that I didn't know how to match the right colors together, so I just started wearing mostly black and white! I began wearing a little makeup but was still unsure about how to apply and what colors were best.

"I wish I had this information long ago!

"This course has really taught me how to bring out my beauty. I now love accessorizing! And I can't believe the comfort and confidence I feel now. I used to feel so unsure, especially when I dressed up, but now I feel beautiful and sophisticated. I feel so good about myself and who I am when I am dressing my truth, and, yes, shopping is more fun, too! What I love the best though, is looking in my closet and seeing all the colors harmonize, and knowing that everything in there is comfortable and looks good on me!

"You've made dressing fun (finally!) Thank you Carol for all you do. I've read all your books and listened to most of your audio content. You are an important spiritual teacher in my life."

Move forward now in *Dressing Your Truth®* and you will discover an amazing world of natural, easy-to-achieve beauty that awaits you!

God bless you! You were created to be beautiful!

Shopping Your Truth—10 Great Rules

AFTER YOU HAVE LEARNED TO DRESS YOUR TRUTH, you can confidently use these 10 rules for shopping to create easy, affordable, and incredibly successful shopping trips.

1. **DECIDE HOW YOU LIKE TO SHOP**. Type 1s usually prefer to go with friends and make it a fun, social event. Type 2s prefer to make it a more intimate one-on-one experience with one other friend, or go by themselves so they don't feel pressured. Type 3s are the swiftest shoppers, getting in and out of the stores fast, so they should go alone or with someone that can keep up. Type 4s prefer to go alone, and if they are with someone, prefer not to be told what they should buy or even look at.

2. **COLORS**. When looking for clothes that are true to your Type, first look for your color. You can scan the racks quickly to spot your colors. Next, see if the garment has the other four elements that are true to your Type. Use the style guide that comes with your *Dressing Your Truth®* course.

3. **LOVE IT OR LEAVE IT**. You have to be able to say "I love it." If you cannot say "I love it," put it back! Only buy items you absolutely love and know you will wear again and again. Remember, this is a process. Be patient with your learning.

4. **LISTEN TO YOUR BODY**. The more you Dress Your Truth, the more your body will "feel" what is right for you. Take time to try on what you are thinking of buying. Your body will tell you if it is right for you. If it doesn't feel right, put it back.

5. **TREASURE HUNTING**. I don't go to the mall or conventional retail stores often. I have fun shopping outside the conventional retail world because I like the challenge of finding great stuff at thrift and consignment stores. In fact, I find my best pieces at consignment and thrift stores—where I get 60 to 70 percent of my wardrobe. I love to go treasure hunting for great fashion at these stores. Because you are outside the conventional retail world, you have more options since consignment and thrift stores are not stocking only the latest styles and trends.

6. **STYLE VS. TYPE**. Only wear what is "in style" if it is right for your Type. Some current styles may be perfect for you; otherwise, just pass them by. Remember: you will always look stylish if you are dressing your truth.

7. **CREATE AN ABUNDANT, AFFLUENT MIND-SET**. Do you think to yourself, "I can never find what I want," or "It is hard to find things that fit me," or, "I can never find what I want at a price I can afford!"? Your beliefs create your reality, and if these are your beliefs, that will be your experience. Change your shopping beliefs to thoughts like this "I always find great pieces at great prices," and "Shopping is easy for me, I always find great deals," and (I love this one), "I have the best luck finding things I love that fit me perfectly." It works and you will be amazed what shows up for you. My mother often says about me, "Carol just has the best luck when she shops, the clothes just fly off the rack when she walks in!" Hmm. Mom, could that be because I believe they will?

8. **THE HUSBAND RULE**. Only take your husband or boyfriend or whoever shopping if he/she supports you and has fun. Otherwise, leave him home!

9. **BUDGET**. Know what you can invest in and establish your shopping budget before you go.

10. **ONLINE TOOLS**. We've discovered that many of our clients are finding the best results with their *Dressing Your Truth*® experience by utilizing the tools we've created to make it easy. Take a look at the *Dressing Your Truth*® Online Store at www.dressingyourtruth.com/shop/. This store was specifically created to offer you hair care products, all aspects of makeup and skincare, jewelry and more, all by Type!

PAY IT FORWARD

YOU ARE TRULY AMAZING! You bring light, joy and excitement to the world! Keep moving forward in this new-found you! It will only get better as the weeks go on.

Dressing Your Truth® brings the true you out! When you are dressing your truth, you are literally wearing you on your clothes. You are a beautiful woman and that is what your outer appearance will be saying about you to the world! You are a gift of light and joy to the world—so let that be known!

Living your truth and *Dressing Your Truth®* is a gift to the world. I am sure by this time other women have noticed the change in you!

Some may have asked you, "What are you doing? You look fantastic!" Others may not have said anything, but believe me, they are noticing.

> WOMEN HAVE BEEN TAUGHT TO SETTLE FOR MEDIOCRITY WHEN IT COMES TO THEIR BODIES AND THEIR BEAUTY.

Women have been taught to settle for mediocrity when it comes to their bodies and their beauty, having been taught superficial methods by the fashion industry that actually camouflages most women's beauty.

Think for a moment about a woman you know, even a teen girl you know who would love to know about *Dressing Your Truth®*. Maybe it's your sister, your neighbor, your mom, maybe even your own daughter.

Take the time to introduce them to the *Beauty Profile*^SM system and *Dressing Your Truth*®. What a gift you are giving them. Especially a teen girl—wow, think of the years saved from shameful dressing room experiences and negative views of herself and body.

My greatest hope is that, if you are a mother, you will guide your daughters to this information so they can become their own beauty experts early their life, before they fall victim to the whims, styles and trends of the fashion industry. And if your daughters are between the ages of 12–18, and you teach them the truth about their beauty and support them in learning how to dress their truth, quite possibly we could revolutionize the fashion industry within a couple of generations!

Dressing Your Truth® is a priceless gift. If you share this revolutionary system with the women you know, they will bless you and thank you.

A Message to Teen Girls

THE DOVE SELF-ESTEEM FUND recently commissioned a study entitled *Real Girls, Real Pressure: A National Report on the State of Self-Esteem* that addressed the self-esteem crisis in the United States that encompasses nearly every aspect of a girl's life, including her perception of her looks, her academic performance, and her relationships with family and friend. Participants in the study were girls aged 8 through 17. (See it at *content.dove.us/makeadiff/ pdf/SelfEsteem_Report.pdf*.)

The study offers some key findings that are very telling about what is going on in a young girl's head. For example, an astounding 70 percent of girls believe they are not good enough and don't measure up in some way. Of girls with low self-esteem, 75 percent said they participated in negative activities such as eating disorders, bullying and cutting themselves.

It's clear to me that we can do a lot more than we are doing to stem the tide of low self-esteem among teen girls in our midst.

Here's a case in point. A short time ago, I encountered a young woman who was dressed so immodestly that she inspired me to create one of my latest video blog posts which I affectionately titled, "Your Beauty Is in Your Face, Not in Your Boobs." I invite you to watch this video at www.thecarolblog.com.

Really, it took everything in me to bite my Type 3 tongue and keep from saying something. This young lady did not even have much to share with the world, but she was doing all she could do to share it. I could tell she lacked confidence and had an emptiness inside. She was searching for acceptance outside of herself, when actually she can only find it within herself.

Girls, listen to me on this one. The media and fashion world has sexualized beauty to make you think looking sexy is what feminine beauty is. Looking sexy and pretty is not about showing your cleavage and other parts of your body.

When I was your age, the only women I knew that wore push-up bras were Zsa-Zsa and Eva Gabor! (You probably don't know who they are—ask your mom.) Nowadays, almost all teenage girls own a push-up bra. My point is, there is way too much attention put on a woman's breasts as being the most attractive part of her.

Your mom may want you to dress modestly for moral reasons and to not turn guys heads! As a mom, that is a good reason, but my reason for telling you to cover your breasts and tummy is not to keep you from attracting the wrong kind of guy, it is to tell you that it's just not your best look! If you want to be incredibly beautiful, think again about how much skin you are willing to reveal.

> YOU CAN'T PUT ON SELF-CONFIDENCE AND SELF-LOVE.

I believe that your greatest beauty is in your smile and your eyes. Your smile radiates what is in your heart—your personality and who you truly are. Your eyes are the window to your soul, and they shine forth your light and beauty from within. Your face holds your greatest beauty. Why? Because it reveals who you really are like nothing else can.

You can't put on self-confidence or self-love. You "wear" what you believe about yourself, no matter what kind of clothes you have on. That's what tells your true story, and that's why you need to learn the truth. Learn to Dress Your Truth as early as you can in life, and avoid the painful experiences too many of us older woman have lived with for many unhappy years.

Another thing: stop telling yourself you are not beautiful or that you are fat. You will only create what you don't want when you hold that belief! Stop shaming yourself when you look in the mirror. Stop comparing yourself to other girls and deeming yourself less adequate. Stop thinking you will never be pretty or thin enough. When you learn to fully accept yourself, none of these phrases will make any sense to you anymore.

Don't look to celebrities and fashion magazines to decide which fashions are right for you. I am sure you are aware that all the images of girls and women in fashion magazines are doctored by photo manipulation and airbrushing.

I have the good fortune to be the mother of two amazing daughters, Jennifer (Type 1) and Anne (Type 2). At the time of this writing, Jenny is 28, and Anne is 24. Both my girls learned to dress their truth early in life. I don't think either one of them has ever had the thought that they were not pretty enough. My daughters-in-law, Sarah, age 26 (Type 3), and Jaleah, age 22 (a Type 1), are both fine examples of very beautiful young women. Anne and Sarah are our lead *Dressing Your Truth*® trainers and both play a big role in teaching teen girls how to live their truth and love themselves. Be an example to your peers and lead the way in claiming your truth by learning what Type of young woman you are, and then choosing to live your truth on the inside and out! When you understand the truth about the real source of your own beauty, it will show in your smile, your eyes and in every aspect of your being. And people will notice you like never before, not for your immodest dress, but for your real beauty—the real you!

I invite you, your friends, and your mother to share this journey with me. You'll be so happy that you did!

Top Celebs Dressing Their Truth

I'VE LISTED HERE A NUMBER OF CELEBRITIES, some who are naturally dressing their truth. Although they may not always be right on target, they seem to be following their intuitive sense of what is true to their Type and are making consistent choices that are right for their Type of beauty.

CELEBS DRESSING THEIR TRUTH

These women are successful at dressing their truth, although they could use a little help here and there to bring their look into complete integrity with their Type:

- Ellen Degeneres, Type1—Ellen has a clean, crisp, fresh look that is true to her buoyant, upbeat nature. Her hair always looks great for her Type as well.

- Goldie Hawn, Type 1—Goldie wears gold highlights, has big bounce in her hair, and wears bright colors .

- Jennifer Aniston, Type 2—Jennifer has flowing, layered hair, and uses soft tones which honor her natural softness.

- Hillary Clinton, Type 2—Hillary does a great job with her Type 2 hairstyle which is perfect for her.

- Barbra Streisand, Type 2— Barbara wears flowing, soft garments. Her hair is soft and flows inward, true to her Type 2 nature.

- Joan Rivers, Type 3— Joan wears a lot of edgy styles, puts angles around her face, has a great Type 3 hairstyle, and wears substantial jewelry.

- Ashlee Simpson, Type 3—Ashlee wears rich colors and has an edgy look.

- Anne Hathaway, Type 4—Anne wears bold colors, including lip color. She has dark hair, and dresses her truth in a simple, sleek way.

- Cher, Type 4—True to her Type, Cher has been making bold statements with her attire for many years!

- Gwen Stefani, Type 4—Gwen is a platinum blonde. She displays high contrast, has bold lips and a bold style.

- Ivanka Trump, Type 4—Donald Trump's daughter Ivanka has a sleek, stylized look, and dresses in a simple yet classic manner.

- Kourtney Kardashian, Type 4—Kourtney wears her hair long and straight, with a middle part. She wears a lot of black and solid colors.

My Parting Thoughts

THERE IS ONE LAST THOUGHT I WANT TO LEAVE YOU WITH. *Don't feel guilty for giving this to yourself!* Did you hear that? Do I need to be more clear? ***Do not, I repeat, do not feel guilty for giving this to yourself!***

You may be one of too many women who have feelings of guilt come up when you start to give attention to yourself, and especially your looks. Investing in your appearance can cause guilt due to the belief that doing so is vain and worldly.

Think about it: I feel you would agree that this is an archaic, out-dated, backwards belief that is no longer serving women. As women continue to evolve, to know their truth and live it, having the belief that I am incredibly beautiful inside and out can no longer be considered a vain, conceited way to view yourself. Every mother wants her daughter to know and believe this!

Remember: a mom cannot teach a daughter what she does not believe herself. At a deep level you have always believed you are beautiful inside and out. You just temporarily bought into the lie that you were not beautiful, and I know that because if it were true, you would not have been led to this information to once again unveil that truth to yourself.

This is a no-brainer to me. If a woman loves herself, feels good about herself and once and for all puts to rest the inner and outer battle with her body and appearance, you are going to see some pretty far reaching effects. Women who love themselves are better moms, wives, employers, employees, friends, leaders and neighbors. I guarantee that this world needs a lot more women living and dressing their truth, and when that change happens, we will see generations change. I truly believe that.

Women are the heartbeat of humanity and when a woman knows and lives her truth, she has a far-reaching, even vast effect.

You are not being selfish, vain, worldly or self-centered by taking an interest in your appearance and beauty. You are simply loving yourself and showing other women how to more fully love themselves.

In her book *Return to Love*, Marianne Williamson said, "Our deepest fear is not that we are inadequate. Our deepest fear is that we are powerful beyond measure. It is our light, not our darkness that most frightens us. We ask ourselves, 'Who am I to be brilliant, gorgeous, talented, fabulous?' Actually, who are you not to be? You are a child of God. Your playing small does not serve the world. There is nothing enlightened about shrinking so that other people won't feel insecure around you. We are all meant to shine, as children do. We were born to make manifest the glory of God that is within us. It's not just in some of us; its in everyone. And as we let our own light shine, we unconsciously give other people permission to do the same. As we are liberated from our own fear, our presence automatically liberates others."

If that fear comes up for you, stand up to that limiting belief and tell yourself that it is a belief that has never served women. Replace it with your new belief, "I am loving myself and living my truest self. I love how I look and feel and honor my God-given beauty."

Go for it! I love you and thank you for letting me help you along your journey. As we continue to awaken to our feminine truth and live it, God will enable us to bless the lives of many more women.

It is the time of a feminine awakening. As a spiritual and metaphysical teacher, I have known this for years. Who knew that the feminine awakening would also include beauty and fashion. It makes great sense! Creating consciousness in the beauty and fashion world is a role I am happy to play. Thanks for supporting me.

I love you,

Carol Tuttle

Part 8

- RESOURCES

- ABOUT THE AUTHOR

RESOURCES

THE FOLLOWING RESOURCES WILL SUPPORT YOU IN DRESSING YOUR TRUTH® AND HONORING YOUR TYPE OF BEAUTY. Living true to your Type doesn't just affect your appearance. As these resources will show you, living true to your Type can support you in creating stronger relationships, better health, more money, and a happier family. *Enjoy.*

DRESSING YOUR TRUTH

At www.dressingyourtruth.com, you will find a beautifully designed website where you can purchase the *Dressing Your Truth®* course for your Type of beauty. There are four separate 3-hour interactive online courses, one for each Type of women.

When you purchase an online course, you'll also enjoy membership in the *Dressing Your Truth®* Club and be eligible to attend our exclusive regularly scheduled Club Nights either live or online. You also have access to our Club Night Video Vault where you continue your learning on how to create your own personal style for your Type.

Your online experience also includes access to our hair image gallery and our constantly growing gallery of different looks and outfits where you will find help on how to Dress Your Truth in any setting, from stay-at-home mom to the professional woman. And for all the women who have been spending hours straightening your curly hair, we help you fall in love with your curly hair and bring our your best look with our special Perfect Curly Hair module for every Type of woman. You'll enjoy interaction with other women who are dressing their truth through our community forums, where you can support each other in this one-of-a-kind, fun and empowering experience. We are continuing to develop resources to enable you to become your own beauty expert.

Take the next step and start your *Dressing Your Truth®* online experience now at *www.dressingyourtruth.com*.

IT'S JUST MY NATURE!

For a more detailed study of Carol's *Energy Profiling®* system—the origin of her *Beauty Profiling*SM system—we recommend Carol's book, *It's Just My Nature!* Carol teaches in her typical entertaining and practical style the principles of her *Energy Profiling®* system and provides additional information that will help you use this assessment tool to better understand your family and friends. We encourage you to introduce the *Energy Profiling®* program to your spouse, companion, children, other loved ones and friends. Thousands of *Energy Profiling®* system users have expressed how understanding each other's Type has dramatically improved the quality of their relationships. Please visit www.myenergyprofile. com to find Carol's book and more support materials to learn about the *Energy Profiling®* system.

THE CAROL BLOG

The Carol Blog offers a fun and entertaining resource for continuing to learn about topics including *Dressing Your Truth®*, More *Energy Profiling®* information, and Living Your Truth. Carol's engaging and candid style is captured in her frequent written and video blog posts. The Carol Blog also features hundreds of *Dressing Your Truth®* Before & After photos, where you can see for yourself the amazing results for every Type of beauty. Visit the Carol Blog today at www.thecarolblog.com.

CAROL TUTTLE HEALING RESOURCES

As a 20-year pioneer in the personal development and alternative health fields, Carol Tuttle has created a wide array of resources to help you heal your life. At The Carol Tuttle Healing Center, you will find online video and audio sessions with Carol to help you heal from low self-esteem, relationship issues, weight and body issues, abuse and other life challenges. Carol also offers some of the best multi-media home study courses, CDs, DVDs to help you create more abundance and joy in areas of self, health, money and relationships. We highly recommend Carol's best-selling book, *Remembering Wholeness: A Personal Handbook for Thriving in the 21st Century*, that has already helped tens of thousands of people live their divine truth and create lives of joy and prosperity. For these resources please visit www.caroltuttle.com.

WEBSITES REFERENCED IN THIS BOOK

DRESSING YOUR TRUTH®:
www.dressingyourtruth.com

DRESSING YOUR TRUTH® ONLINE STORE:
www.dressingyourtruth.com/shop

CAROL'S BLOG:
www.thecarolblog.com

THE *ENERGY PROFILING®* SYSTEM:
www.myenergyprofile.com

CAROL'S HOME SITE:
www.caroltuttle.com

THE CAROL TUTTLE HEALING CENTER:
www.youremotionalhealing.com

MANIFESTING MORE MONEY:
If you need support for clearing your patterns of lack and scarcity with money, as mentioned in an earlier section of this book, we recommend Carol's home study course, Manifesting More Money. This course will help you identify where you're blocked with allowing more money into your life and will teach you the vital steps to increasing your wealth. Learn more at *www.manifestingmoremoney.com*

THE CHILD WHISPERER
Carol's latest book is the ultimate handbook for raising happy, successful, cooperative children. By applying each of the 4 Types to the experience of parenting, she teaches parents how to eliminate tantrums, motivate children, and use less discipline, all by parenting children true to their natures. Learn more at *thechildwhisperer.com*

About the Author

BEST-SELLING AUTHOR AND ACCLAIMED ALTERNATIVE PSYCHO-THERAPIST CAROL TUTTLE has turned her attention to the beauty and fashion world. As a result of Carol's research of the how the current fashion system defeats women and adds to issues of low  self-esteem and negative body image, Carol designed a revolutionary do-it-yourself beauty makeover system called *Dressing Your Truth®* that is changing the fashion and beauty industries. *Dressing Your Truth®* is empowering women to make fashion and beauty choices, not just according to trends, but in harmony with their personal Type of beauty—their inner truth.

Dressing Your Truth® provides women with simple beauty and fashion assessments, quickly helping them tap into their natural beauty and way of being. They learn to express the true nature of who they are—their purpose and passions, and even their physical features—in perfect harmony with their clothing, jewelry, hair color and style.

Carol has appeared on over 150 radio and television talk shows, providing pioneering insights on weight, fashion/beauty, sex, intimacy and relationships, depression, self-esteem, parenting, finances, physical health and spiritual health. Her media appearances include features in national print, TV and radio.

As a bestselling author, Carol is a personal development pioneer and motivator. For the last 20 years, she has devoted her life to helping people rise out of deprivation to living lives of abundance.

Carol is the author of the acclaimed self-help book *Remembering Wholeness: A Personal Handbook for Thriving* in *the 21st Century*, which made her a best-selling author, selling over 77,000 copies to date with sales continuing to rise mainly through word-of-mouth popularity.

Carol is the Founder of Living Your Truth in Lehi, Utah. Carol and her husband Jonathan reside in Utah and are the parents of five children. Carol's entire family lives their truth and dresses it, even their Type 2 dog Jocco!